**New Directions for
Teaching and Learning**

Catherine M. Wehlburg
EDITOR-IN-CHIEF

D1522492

Inclusive Teaching: Presence in the Classroom

Cornell Thomas

EDITOR

Number 140 • Winter 2014
Jossey-Bass
San Francisco

INCLUSIVE TEACHING: PRESENCE IN THE CLASSROOM
Cornell Thomas (ed.)
New Directions for Teaching and Learning, no. 140
Catherine M. Wehlburg, Editor-in-Chief

Microfilm copies of issues and articles are available in 16 mm and 35 mm, as well as microfiche in 105 mm, through University Microfilms, Inc., 300 North Zeeb Road, Ann Arbor, MI 48106-1346.

NEW DIRECTIONS FOR TEACHING AND LEARNING (ISSN 0271-0633, electronic ISSN 1536-0768) is part of The Jossey-Bass Higher and Adult Education Series and is published quarterly by Wiley Subscription Services, Inc., A Wiley Company, at Jossey-Bass, One Montgomery Street, Suite 1200, San Francisco, CA 94104-4594. POSTMASTER: Send address changes to New Directions for Teaching and Learning, Jossey-Bass, One Montgomery Street, Suite 1200, San Francisco, CA 94104-4594.

New Directions for Teaching and Learning is indexed in CIJE: Current Index to Journals in Education (ERIC), Contents Pages in Education (T&F), Educational Research Abstracts Online (T&F), ERIC Database (Education Resources Information Center), Higher Education Abstracts (Claremont Graduate University), and SCOPUS (Elsevier).

INDIVIDUAL SUBSCRIPTION RATE (in USD): $89 per year US/Can/Mex, $113 rest of world; institutional subscription rate: $335 US, $375 Can/Mex, $409 rest of world. Single copy rate: $29. Electronic only–all regions: $89 individual, $335 institutional; Print & Electronic–US: $98 individual, $402 institutional; Print & Electronic–Can/Mex: $98 individual, $442 institutional; Print & Electronic–rest of world: $122 individual, $476 institutional.

Cover design: Wiley
Cover Images: © Lava 4 images | Shutterstock

EDITORIAL CORRESPONDENCE should be sent to the editor-in-chief, Catherine M. Wehlburg, c.wehlburg@tcu.edu.

www.josseybass.com

CONTENTS

FROM THE SERIES EDITOR

About This Publication

Since 1980, *New Directions for Teaching and Learning* (NDTL) has brought a unique blend of theory, research, and practice to leaders in postsecondary education. NDTL sourcebooks strive not only for solid substance but also for timeliness, compactness, and accessibility.

The series has four goals: to inform readers about current and future directions in teaching and learning in postsecondary education, to illuminate the context that shapes these new directions, to illustrate these new directions through examples from real settings, and to propose ways in which these new directions can be incorporated into still other settings.

This publication reflects the view that teaching deserves respect as a high form of scholarship. We believe that significant scholarship is conducted not only by researchers who report results of empirical investigations but also by practitioners who share disciplinary reflections about teaching. Contributors to NDTL approach questions of teaching and learning as seriously as they approach substantive questions in their own disciplines, and they deal not only with pedagogical issues but also with the intellectual and social context in which these issues arise. Authors deal on the one hand with theory and research and on the other with practice, and they translate from research and theory to practice and back again.

About This Volume

This volume focuses on the importance of inclusive teaching and the role faculty can play in helping students achieve by adjusting their approach to teaching by believing that each student has the ability to learn, though not necessarily in the same way. The authors in this volume embrace the ideals of inclusive teaching and believe that most, if not all, learners become actively engaged in their own learning in settings where inclusive teaching take place. Faculty today are faced with a much more diverse student body each year. While some colleges and universities address this trend by adjusting entry requirements, others do not have this option and this challenge must be met in the classroom by caring faculty who trust that all students can and will learn and that all students bring different aspects of their lives to the learning environment. To teach with a focus on inclusivity means that most, if not all, individuals want to learn, to improve their ability to better understand the world in which they live, and to be able to navigate their pathways of life.

Catherine M. Wehlburg
Editor-in-Chief

*In a real teaching and learning community of learners, the belief
exists that all can and will learn, that the teacher has the ability to
connect new information with the knowledge base of each student,
and that students will become empowered to make their own
connections. This premise is built on a foundation that sees each
student as a unique human being with the ability to grow. They are
not cloaked by some set of generalized characteristics. They are not
invisible.*

No Longer Invisible

Cornell Thomas

Introduction

The thoughts presented in this chapter address the concerns many of us
have concerning the academic preparation and acumen of learners matric-
ulating to institutions of higher education.

> A larger proportion of the population than ever before are participating in
> some form of postsecondary education—but college access and completion
> remain inadequate for traditionally underserved groups, especially the poor,
> ethnic minorities, and older students. The increased share of college costs
> being borne by individuals, so far without a similar increase in financial aid
> for underserved groups or in improved public school preparation for them,
> continues this disparity. (Zusman 2005, 160)

Following is an exercise that will uncloak some of the perceptual barriers currently impeding our path leading to more student academic success.
Once the reader immerses himself/herself in this exercise, it will become
evident that I am proposing a different philosophical platform upon which
we think, act, and teach. It is my hope that you embrace this new platform
and help make it so.

As you read the chapter, you will see that I am suggesting that there
are ways for educators to utilize certain teaching and learning techniques to
improve the academic growth of these underserved students. These efforts
will help increase both retention and graduation rates. I am also suggesting

NEW DIRECTIONS FOR TEACHING AND LEARNING, no. 140, Winter 2014 © 2014 Wiley Periodicals, Inc.
Published online in Wiley Online Library (wileyonlinelibrary.com) • DOI: 10.1002/tl.20108

that teaching and learning environments that help learners to connect their personal knowledge with the information we want them to learn have the potential to dramatically increase student success.

The concept of inquiry learning will be briefly examined to illustrate one method that will increase students' academic growth. This concept will then be paired with Parker Palmer's (2011, 44–45) five habits of the heart:

1. We must understand that we are all in this together.
2. We must develop an appreciation of the value of "otherness."
3. We must cultivate the ability to hold tension in life-giving ways.
4. We must generate a sense of personal voice and agency.
5. We must strengthen our capacity to create community.

Palmer's habits of the heart will allow each of us to explore the possibilities for positive change and challenge us to rethink our perceptions regarding some of the students we teach. The intent of this chapter is to introduce to some, and remind others of, a pathway leading to more inclusive, engaging, and successful teaching and learning environments.

Dreaming?

I have had a reoccurring dream over the past few years. In this dream, educators understand that culture is an individual phenomenon. These educators understand that each learner's experiences are their own. They are unique. While some learners have similar foundational values and historical traditions, some new experiences can, and often do, have a major impact on how one thinks and therefore acts. These kinds of experiences cause an individual to change their actions, values, and even their sense of self. Through experiences one becomes a different individual, a changed individual, and an even more unique soul ready for even more growth as they live and imagine the possibilities in their life.

In this dream, educators no longer group together individuals by using generalizations (race, gender, social economic status, ethnicity, religion, sexual orientation, and so on). These and other generalizations have been employed historically to justify the treatment of people in this country who were considered different from full access to the American Dream. The results of these generalizations in institutions of learning have proven disastrous. However, in my dream, we form new sets of thinking that see each of us as a unique being with the potential for great growth. In my dream, educators know that all of us learn better and understand more deeply when we can connect new information with the things we already know. In my dream, learners take control of their learning and educators act more as facilitators. Or, is this more of a dream deferred (Hughes 1994) with no chance of becoming reality?

NEW DIRECTIONS FOR TEACHING AND LEARNING • DOI: 10.1002/tl

Filters

Max Stirner talks about "Wheels in the Head." He refers to a thought that a person cannot give up as a "Wheel in the Head," which in turn controls an individual's will and uses the individual rather than being used by the individual. Are these Wheels similar to the social constructs in this society that allow negative stereotypic images of people control what we think of them and tell some of us our potential for success based merely on our perceived race or social economic status? Are these Wheels similar to the social constructs in this society that provide the rationales some educators employ to justify remedial programs, tracking, rote teaching processes, and high stakes testing? Are these Wheels similar to the social constructs in this society that have created gatekeepers (IQ tests and entrance level exams) that limit entrance for so many individuals in our society into the ivory towers of higher education? I would suggest that they do. (Thomas 2013, 6)

Many of us grew up in families learning to understand a set of values that distinguished right from wrong, good from bad, smart from dumb, strong from weak, pretty from ugly, and acceptance from rejection. Sharing was a right thing to do, while selfishness was bad. Following directions from your parents and teachers was a good thing to do, but hitting your sibling was bad. You were rewarded for the smart things that you did, and punished for your actions that were considered dumb. The books utilized in our school, along with major media outlets, helped to create the image of the strong American leader. This person was typically male, tall, lean, and with a skin color most classify as white in our society. Women were shown to be the weaker sex. People of color were depicted in ways that told us these people were less intelligent, lacked leadership or even self-sufficiency skills, and were better suited to be followers and servants. Much of the success during the first nearly 200 years of our great nation supported these depictions.

One of the most comprehensive efforts to deal with racial-national questions in biological evolutionary terms was made by Nathaniel S. Shaler. Previously vague and romantic notions of Anglo-Saxon peoplehood, combined with general ethnocentrism, rudimentary wisps of genetics, selected tidbits of evolutionary theory, and naive assumptions from an early and crude imported anthropology produced the doctrine that the English, Germans, and others of the "old immigration" constituted a superior race of tall, blond, blue-eyed "Nordics" or "Aryans" whereas the people of eastern and southern Europe made up the darker Alpine or Mediterranean—both "inferior" breeds whose presence in America threatened either by inter mixture or supplementation, the traditional American stock and culture. (Livingstone 1984, 181)

New Directions for Teaching and Learning • DOI: 10.1002/tl

These are examples of the images that have helped to form many of our thoughts and beliefs about ourselves and others. These perceptions also help to form in our minds justifications for the disparities, income, career opportunities, access to education and health care, and so on, that we have in our society.

These straightforward examples of treatment based on either/or descriptors are at the root of many of the ills of our society today. Seemingly basic, clear-cut ways of making sense of the world plague our attempts to value anyone who seems to be different. This approach has caused many of us in this society to think of gays, racial groups, non-Christians, and those with a disability, for example, as *less than*. Thinking in this way has led to a sense of alienation for so many citizens in this country and entitlement for others. What is most alarming is that differences are attributed to individuals based merely on socially constructed group identifiers. This way of thinking and acting work as filters designed to justify differentiated treatment of citizens in our great nation.

Filters are mechanisms utilized to block certain objects, substances, or ideologies while allowing others to get through. For example, there are coffee, air, oil, cigarette, water, and soil filters that are designed to separate what is considered to be the bad from the good. Other filters have been designed to work in similar ways. Decisions determining who could vote during the early, and now more recent, history of our country; who would live free or as slave; why we can pay women and people of color less for the same work; and who has access to a quality education are all filters currently in use at varying degrees in our society today. One's social economic status has a great impact on access to, among other things, a quality education, excellent health care, and a clear pathway when determining personal life choices. The use of filtering has created a deficit model approach when developing an understanding about those considered different. It provides justification for the mistreatment of some and for the privileges for others. This process has unfortunately been institutionalized in our society.

> ... if inequity has been institutionalized in the theories, norms, and practices of our society, and if researchers and administrators deify inequity and injustice by failing to examine, question, and redress the inequities they see, then there is much to be done. (Larson and Murtadha 2003, 134)

Is the use of these and other institutionalized filters in concert with the thoughts and beliefs of the signers of our Constitution?

> We hold these truths...

The challenges we face in our education systems can be traced back to these very same filters. The use of filters as described here poses major challenges that we must successfully address if we truly want to create and maintain the kind of highly effective teaching and learning environments that we seek. We must bring to the fore our thoughts and actions in ways to demonstrate the premise that different means less than is no longer our belief. We must turn this ideology of filters and its damage to our society inside out. Stirner (in Spring 1994, 44) suggests a need to transgress from the educated person, where knowledge is the determiner of choice, to the free person, where knowledge is the source of greater choice. This shift in thinking is of major importance if we truly want to improve teaching and learning in this country.

Inquiry Learning

In a quotation, John Dewey states that:

> Inquiry and questioning, up to a certain point, are synonymous terms. We inquire when we question; and we inquire when we seek whatever will provide an answer to a question asked. (Hickman and Alexander 1998, 171)

An inquiry is any process that has as its goal to provide answers that bring clarity to that being questioned. This goal is most often accomplished when existing knowledge and understanding is used to help bring clarity to that being questioned. In other words, the unknown becomes more familiar when it can be compared and contrasted against what is assumed to be known. For example, a learner can bring clarity to notions of social justice in this country by reflecting on their personal experiences and the perceived and/or real barriers that have emerged during their life. Or, simply by combining oil and water to see that it really does not mix! Of course, levels of questioning and inquiry are often much more complex. The point here is that the learner, rather than the teacher or some predetermined set of exclusive ideals, should serve as the starting point of inquiry. The learner, when no longer disempowered to do so, develops his or her own capacity to link/connect what is known with the knowledge sought.

> There must be sincere and *concerted efforts* by educators toward creating conditions for success in every classroom in all of our schools. Educators using techniques to invite the learner into the teaching and learning process demonstrate how valuable these methods of instructional interaction are in creating climates that optimize success. (Thomas 2013, 66)

The learner, by nature, is inquisitive. However, methods of teaching and learning that merely seek the regurgitation of facts eventually discourage learners from using their own ability to raise questions, to inquire, to seek answers, to understand, and to help develop new questions and new meanings. Memorizing facts is an excellent method for low-level learning. But this level of learning is just not enough. Learners must be inquisitive and actively engaged in the pursuit of knowledge. Lectures that require learners to memorize and give what has been memorized back on exams should lead to further inquiry; should raise the question, "why?"; and should fuel the process of learning. The "why" becomes personal. The answers when connected to the personal "why" help the learner to internalize the answers that emerge. When the personal is discouraged, there is a lack of connection between the known and the knowledge being sought. Just imagine trying to cross over the Mississippi River in St. Louis, Missouri, without the use of a bridge. The bridge serves as a connector between where you are and where you want to go. We need similar bridges to connect personal meaning with the information we want our students to learn. Instead, voices are lost and the learner becomes invisible in the teaching and learning process. This lack of connection eventually shuts down the learner's ability, and even sometimes desire, to raise questions; to personalize meaning; and to move teaching and learning from an abstract form to more of a personal, highly engaging, and empowering process. Once again, it is suggested here that memorizing facts and other information is just not enough in today's more globally and inclusively diverse society. This process of teaching and learning does not recognize the individual, and eventually distracts and discourages the learner from fully engaging in anything concerning the formal school experiences. Levels of motivation disappear. The results in our great nation have been disastrous.

> The persistent failure of urban schools and repeated efforts to change them have shaped much of the debate about education policy in the United States over the past forty years. The issues have remained stubbornly constant: inadequate funding and resources, unequal educational opportunities, high dropout rates and low academic achievement, student alienation, racial segregation, and race and class inequality within and among urban schools. (Lipman 2004, 5)

We should all embrace the belief that we have the abilities to help empower learners to construct processes leading to the answers they seek from the questions that emerge instead of only seeking the answers that have filtered out all other opinions, voices, values, and possibilities. This call for connections in the teaching and learning process through inquiry and engagement is crucial to maximizing each learner's academic growth. Teaching and learning environments that embrace these ideals see learners who acquire and analyze information, develop and support propositions, provide possible solutions, and often develop new ways of thinking and understandings. The barriers leading to more empowered learners are eradicated. Learners in these environments take more ownership of their learning. They learn how to learn for themselves. They also share what they learn, becoming teachers.

> When students internalize new information, they connect what is new with something already known and understood. Therefore, experiences connected to new information and existing knowledge help us to understand the importance of learning. Students in this process also experience high levels of success. Through these types of experiences students begin to realize the joy of new learning. Most importantly, students begin to understand and appreciate the value of determining for self what something means. Students begin to thirst for more learning opportunities. Learning is seen and embraced as a life-long journey. Seeking knowledge and understanding becomes an energizing force along a personal and spiritual pathway of life. (Thomas 2013, 6–7)

Two questions immediately come to mind:

- What would it take to make such a dramatic shift in our thinking and actions regarding teaching and learning?
- How can teachers serve more as a facilitator of learning among a community of learners?

The answers to these and other similar questions are found in our hearts. These shifts in thinking and believing can occur as we begin and continue a reflective journey that raises the question, "why?"—what we believe to be good or bad, right or wrong, and intelligent or not. It is suggested here that this reflective journey can begin with a series of conversations exploring Parker Palmer's five habits of the heart as they relate to teaching and learning. Parker Palmer (2011) posits what he calls the five habits of the heart in his book *Healing the Heart of Democracy*. Although Palmer's focus is on the ills in our society, it is suggested here that these habits can be utilized as part of a journey, causing each of us to change and improve the way we engage learners in the teaching and learning process.

> If American democracy fails, the ultimate cause will not be a foreign invasion or the power of big money or the greed and dishonesty of some elected officials or a military coup or the internal communist/socialist/fascist takeover that keeps some Americans awake at night. It will happen because we—you and I—become so fearful of each other, of our differences and of the future, that we unraveled the civic community on which democracy depends, losing our power to resist all that threatens it and call it back to its highest form. (Palmer 2011, 8)

His five habits of the heart have the potential to turn us away from a deficit model approach to teaching and the expected levels of learning.

This new way of thinking, believing, and doing starts with the premise that everyone can learn and that our task is to find ways to make it so. I will list each of Palmer's five habits of the heart and attempt to demonstrate the positive impact that each can have on our beliefs about learners and our ability to help empower most, if not all, of those that we teach.

Our Work Starts with the Heart

1. *We must understand that we are all in this together.*

> If "We the People" are to hold democracy's tensions in ways that reweave the civic community, we must develop habits that allow our hearts to break open and embrace diversity rather than break down and further divide us. (Palmer 2011, 36)

We must have individuals well prepared for leadership, in business, politics, home, and so on, within a more inclusively diverse world if we are to remain one of the strongest nations on this planet. Therefore, we must embrace "We the People" as a citizenry of diverse, energetic, intelligent, and patriotic individuals and do all that we can to prepare them for the unknown just ahead.

2. *We must develop an appreciation of the value of "otherness."*

> The single most important thing teachers can do is explicitly connect the "big story" of the subject with the "little story" of the student's life. Doing so helps us make progress toward two vital educational goals. We accelerate our students' learning of challenging subjects because they all put more energy into pursuing issues they see as related to their own lives. We support their search for meaning and purpose by giving them information, concepts, and critical tools around questions they care about. (Palmer 2011, 125)

For educators, working with students in ways to create for each of them personal connections with the subject matter clearly demonstrates the belief in the value and uniqueness of each individual.

3. *We must cultivate the ability to hold tension in life-giving ways.*

> So a liberal education, which emerges from the heart of the humanistic tradition, emphasizes the ability to look at an issue from all sides, to be comfortable with contradictions and ambiguities, and to honor paradox in thought, speech, and action. Humanism helps us let the tension of opposites open us to new insights. (Palmer 2011, 149)

For educators, this means that questions from students should be seen as attempts to bring personal meaning to the topics being discussed.

It means that we understand that engaged learning activities may veer from the planned path but with the belief that it is part of the journey leading to a deeper, internalized understanding. It also means that we embrace a teaching and learning environment where all are both—teacher and learner.

4. *We must generate a sense of personal voice and agency.*

> A good education is intentional and thoughtful about helping students find an inner orientation toward what is "out there" that will be life-giving for them and the world. In education as well as religion, we must find ways to help people conduct an inner search free of any predetermined outcome while providing them with the guidance and resources they need to conduct it well. As we do so, we will be shaping some of the habits of the heart that make democracy possible. (Palmer 2011, 123)

Our work should empower each individual learner as they strive to bring meaning to who they are. This growing sense of self-identity will help the learner better understand themselves, the world, and how they can have a positive impact in this life. Therefore, our work is enhanced when we move away from generalized notions of the other. Instead, we strive to get to know each of our students as unique beings, and primarily through conversations they also get to know you. We should hold dear the mantra "Imagine the Possibilities" of each learner—then do all that we can to make it so.

> Educators who value imagination have little problem affirming creativity and dynamism. Imagination points us beyond routine and static possibilities. But more than throwing us toward such possibilities, imagination synthesizes. It connects those things that were previously disconnected. Syntheses are creative acts. They represent the creation or births of new pathways, new possibilities, new hopes, and new dreams. (hooks 2010, 59)

5. *We must strengthen our capacity to create community.*

> The founders excluded many men and all women from the "blessings of liberty" and in this sense, America's founding myth is a flat-out lie. On the other hand, the myth expresses an aspiration without which America would not be the nation it is. Our desire to be a nation that honors equality has proved so powerful that we have been compelled to pursue it for nearly two and a half centuries, a task that will continue to occupy us as long as this nation exists. (Palmer 2011, 179)

Can we have better academic success among the students in our classrooms? I submit to you that indeed we can. The turn will occur most often when each of our classes truly becomes a community of learners. In a real teaching and learning community of learners, the belief exists that all can and will learn, that the teacher has the ability to connect new information with the knowledge base of each student, and that students will become empowered to make their own connections.

Positive change will take place as we embrace the habits of the heart from an educational perspective. I challenge each of us to make it so.

References

Hickman, L. A., and T. M. Alexander. 1998. *The Essential Dewey: Ethics, Logic, Psychology*. Bloomington, IN: Indiana University Press.

hooks, b. 2010. *Teaching Critical Thinking: Practical Wisdom*. New York, NY: Taylor & Francis.

Hughes, L. 1994. "Harlem." In *The Collected Poems of Langston Hughes*, edited by A. Rampersad and D. Roessel, 426. New York, NY: Alfred A. Knopf.

Larson, C. L., and K. Murtadha. 2003. "Leadership for Social Justice." In *The Educational Leadership Challenge for the 21st Century*, edited by J. Murphy, 134–160. Chicago, IL: Chicago University Press.

Lipman, P. 2004. *High Stakes Education*. New York, NY: Routledge.

Livingstone, D. 1984. "Science and Society: Nathaniel S. Shaler and Racial Ideology." *Transactions of the Institute of British Geographers* 9 (2): 181–210.

Palmer, P. 2011. *Healing the Heart of Democracy*. San Francisco, CA: Jossey-Bass.

Spring, J. 1994. *Wheels in the Head*. New York, NY: Routledge.

Thomas, C. 2013. *Transgressing Culture Lines*. Dubuque, IA: Kendall Hunt.

Zusman, A. 2005. "Challenges Facing Higher Education in the Twenty-First Century." In *American Higher Education in the Twenty-First Century*, edited by P. G. Altbach, R. O. Berdahl, and P. J. Gumport, 2nd ed., 115–160. Baltimore, MD: The Johns Hopkins University Press.

CORNELL THOMAS currently serves as a professor of educational leadership in the College of Education at Texas Christian University.

NEW DIRECTIONS FOR TEACHING AND LEARNING • DOI: 10.1002/tl

2

This chapter is designed to provide a stimulus for reflective thinking. The intent is to encourage teachers to reflect upon—even question—a teaching methodology that recognizes and builds upon the learning potential inherent in a cacophony of voices, paradoxical worldviews, and divergent ways of personal being. A pedagogical possibility is explored, one that courts creativity, intellectual flexibility, and open-minded dialectical response. The possibility relates to the orchestration of a classroom setting in which previously silent voices—particularly the socially, politically, or culturally silenced—will join the educational chorus. Here is an academic setting where every student is allowed, encouraged, and expected to be personally present in the classroom. Without presence there is diminished self-identity and a negation of authentic personhood. Without authentic conversational interaction, there is reduced possibility of an intentional learning community that is inclusive of diverse voices. To seek the full reality of student presence in a classroom is to open a door that allows the "other" to interact with the "I."

Presence in the Classroom

Don Hufford

The Meaning of *Presence*

Definitions have a way of being less than definitive—except, perhaps, for the one who defines. Frequently, as the novelist Toni Morrison has reminded us, "definitions define the definer rather than the defined" (Morrison 2004, 93). This leads to an awareness that definitions may be the result of perceptions influenced by ideologies and worldviews. There are, of course, those words with transferable definitions, words that are able to permeate the boundaries of different academic disciplines and schools of speculative thought.

The word, *presence*, fits such a category of permeable definitional possibility. Varying uses of the word make possible expressions of both the mystically abstract and the existentially concrete. Christian theologians—Jewish, Protestant, and Catholic—have wrestled with the theological implications and meanings of the word. *Presence* has been explored in various ways by humanistic psychologists and psychotherapists. Existentialist philosophers

New Directions for Teaching and Learning, no. 140, Winter 2014 © 2014 Wiley Periodicals, Inc.
Published online in Wiley Online Library (wileyonlinelibrary.com) • DOI: 10.1002/tl.20109

have connected *presence* to the meaning of personal authenticity, of identity, of freedom and responsibility, and of the process of personal becoming. Sociologists have defined and wrestled with a "sociology of presence." Literary minds have found creative possibility in "presence, that vague but potent Wordsworthian word," which the poet himself termed the "poetic spirit of our human life" (Langbaum 1982, 37). The word is expressive enough to be "redefined"—or reinterpreted—for other purposes in other settings, including the classroom. Perhaps there is such a reality as "pedagogical presence."

But here a caveat is in order. William Hare has cautioned us to "be wary of succinct definitions, especially when dealing with a rich and fertile notion. It has been said that when one feels the need of a good definition, it is a good idea to lie down until the feeling passes" (Hare 1998, 40). And, we have been reminded by the Jewish theologian Abraham Heschel that "in English the phrase that a person has 'a presence' is hard to define" (Heschel 1965, 90). However, in spite of definitional difficulties, *presence* is a "rich and fertile notion" for teachers to reflect upon. Such reflection opens up opportunities for intellectual dialogue, creative teaching possibilities, and perhaps a little interactive give-and-take between academic disciplines.

Pedagogy of Presence

For a teacher to understand—and implement—the concept of a "pedagogy of presence" is to open up possibilities to teach in counterpoint to the empiricist, technocratic, behaviorist mindset that dominates education today. It is to visualize a classroom in which the dominant metaphor is student-as-person (not student-as-product, consumer, human capital, or facts absorbing test taker). In such a classroom, a methodological motto—borrowed from the Greek philosopher, Heraclitus—might well be "teaching is not to fill a pail, but rather to light a flame." To metaphorically "light a flame" requires a *presence*-generated connecting spark. The spark results from the intellectual friction of a mind-meeting-mind encounter between two autonomous individuals. It requires a meeting, but not a merging, of identities.

It is only when the teacher recognizes the reality of diverse individual *identities*—the existential "I's"—that he/she can maximize the possibility of achieving a classroom learning *community*—a communal "we."

Jo Anne Pagano has noted that she has "learned to treat teaching with great respect; it is no innocent pastime ... at issue are fundamental questions of identity and identification" (Pagano 1998, 255). These questions of identity are integral to the reality of *presence* in a classroom. *Presence* is a revelation—a revealing of "who I am." All too often such self-revealing is discouraged or negated by a classroom power structure that preaches the gospel of an *intentional, inclusive* learning community, but fails to "walk the talk." The open expression of individual identity—necessary to a sense of *presence*—can be a challenge to teacher hegemony and to the efficient, orderly, carefully planned dispensing of officially ordained knowledge. To invite student *presence* into the classroom is risky business. It is to say: be who you are. Express a sense of self. Ask questions, not just of content, but of meaning, purpose, instructional method, and classroom philosophy. Be a vital part of a classroom dialectic. Bring the expressive, lived reality of your existentially authentic racial/cultural/political/economic self into this learning community.

In such a classroom, dialogical encounters are encouraged, and there are violations of the traditional behavioristic boundaries defining an epistemology of "how we learn." Teacher authority and expertise are demystified. The student becomes a coteacher/learner, an equal partner in the adventure of intellectual exploration. The practice of a "pedagogy of presence" requires a teacher who does not demand conditioned consistency, predictability, and inviolable, scripted lesson plans. Such a teacher

> will not remain safely behind the barriers of his own convictions and assurances but will venture forth … It involves us in unforeseen outcomes and unpremeditated conclusions … It gives us the capacity and readiness for exposure. (Hazelton 1960, 57–58)

This venturing teacher—the one who goes forth and who risks exposure and unplanned intellectual adventures—is the one who is *authentically present* in the classroom. Perhaps Soren Kierkegaard was correct:

> A person can distress the spirit by venturing *too little* … To venture is the foundation of inspiration … A bold venture is not a high-flown phase, not an exclamatory outburst, but arduous work. A bold venture, no matter how rash, is not a boisterous proclamation, but a quiet dedication. (Kierkegaard 1999, 398)

It is only by way of the "arduous work and quiet dedication" of an *authentic self* that a teacher can model the kind of "vital presence" that encourages self-revelatory reciprocity on the part of the student (Wexler 1996). Such a teacher has—in the words of Paul Tillich—"the courage to be"—"the courage to be a part of the progress of the group to which he belongs" (Tillich 1961, 109). The group in this case is, of course, the learning community in which teacher/student *mutual presence* is both a process *and* a goal.

> The presence established between myself and another self can be extended to include other persons, so that my awareness will move out from me, as a center of divergence, to the others, and back from the others to me as a force of convergence. This *mutual presence* will establish the community. (Micallef 1969, 22)

It is a sense of *mutual presence*—an intellectual/emotional connecting of teacher and students—that allows a classroom of individuals to become an *inclusive* learning community. It is only when *presence* is shared that there can be a communal "we" in "dialogical communion." Here the term dialogical communion—as it relates to classroom sharing—is symbolic of bell hooks's understanding of "the notion of community, which is like sharing and breaking bread together, of dialogue and mercy ... with a community of faith, not necessarily a religious community, but a community of comrades" (hooks and West 1991, 1–2). Both the religious community and the educational classroom hold the possibility of this kind of dialogical, communal sharing resulting in a sense of comradeship. The one involves a shared religious faith, and the other involves a shared educational quest. In both cases, a Kierkegaardian "leap of faith" is required to establish authentic communion/community. To be *present* is to open oneself to the community.

Martin Buber believed that such a "communion in education ... means being opened up and drawn in" (Buber 1965, 91). To "open up" is to speak up, to communicate a personal reality, to be a *presence* in the classroom. To be "drawn in" is to become part of the learning community, to contribute to its intellectual, emotional, and social—even spiritual—health. It is to listen, to share, to be involved, and to communicate. And, as Thomas Merton has reminded us: "the deepest level of communication is [in] communion ... We discover a new unity ... what we have to be is [who] we are" (Merton 1973, 308). It is, of course, "communication" that opens up the possibility for two or more individuals, being authentic in *who they are*, to find the "we-ness" of communion in a learning community. Rollo May has written that

> communication recovers the original "we-ness" of the human being on a new level. Authentic talk is organic—the speaker ... speaks not as a disembodied voice but as one organic totality to another. (May 1976, 247)

It is through organic communication that *presence* is verified. *Presence* has a metaphysical quality in that it is the communication of individual reality. This communication requires participation, and "participation in the human conversation requires face-to-face relationships and considerable willingness to subject one's views to a cacophony of voices" (Goodlad and Soder 1996, 107). A classroom in which *presence* is sought and welcomed values an inclusive, dialectical cacophony of voices. Intellectual, even emotional, cacophony—open challenges, questions, strongly opposing views, and dynamic interchanges—may shake up classroom decorum, but may also be a prelude to intellectual reflection and personal growth. As John Sullivan has noted: "The existential conditions of the pursuit of truth are such that disagreement, rather than agreement, is generally regarded as the mark of health and competence" (Sullivan 1977, 206).

NEW DIRECTIONS FOR TEACHING AND LEARNING • DOI: 10.1002/tl

When we encourage *presence* in the classroom, we welcome a creative dialectic of disagreement, and divergent voices will be heard. The disagreements themselves will open doors to learning opportunities. Consider Martin Buber's advice that "the teacher must never forget that conflicts too, if only they are decided in a healthy atmosphere, have an educational value" (Buber 1965, 107). It is through the interplay of conversational give-and-take that differing views become educational opportunities, and it is through a "pedagogy of *presence*" that conversation becomes a teaching methodology. Vicki Bergkamp has written that

> the aim of conversation is not to reach a conclusion or agreement; the aim of conversation is the fair airing of views. Conversation is allowing each person and his/her opinions to be recognized ... True conversation is dialectic; it is interchange, a complex set of interactions in which each person works with ideas and convictions and is changed through the interaction. (Bergkamp 2000, 6)

Authentic conversation is not one way; it is interactive, sharing, open-ended, and often provocative. It facilitates intellectual and emotional encounter. It connects ideas *and* people, heads and hearts. Authentic conversation in a classroom requires student/teacher *presence*. What I know, how I interpret my knowledge, and how I express it are authenticated by being filtered through a question that helps define the meaning of personal *presence*: "who am I?"

> In dialogue the quality of the personal experience will be determined by the extent to which participants are encouraged to speak the words which express their deepest authentic understanding of the reality of the truth that they possess ... Such a faithful approach can help transform *individual* participation into *personal* participation, and *collective* experience into *communal* experience. (Del Prete 1990, 155)

The We of Mutual Presence: An Intentional, Inclusive Community

In theological terminology, the communal experience is the *koinonia,* a community of persons in a unique religious relationship to each other (Bohm 1993). There is a semantic connection here to the classroom learning community. In both cases, the goal is a community that has a unified centeredness, one that is more than the sum of its parts, but at the same time maintains unique individual identities. In Soren Kierkegaard's words, "community is certainly more than a sum, yet is truly a sum of ones" (Kierkegaard 1999, 241).

Randolph Miller has defined such an environment: "The I–thou relationship has been achieved, at least for the moment. Thus, the class has become a unity, a group, without the loss of individuality" (Miller 1982, 34). Miller borrows here from Martin Buber's classic concept, which distinguishes between an "I–it" and an "I–thou" relationship. Translated into a classroom situation, an I–it relationship is one in which the student is manipulated as an *object* of the teacher's technical skill and expertise. The teacher (the subject) gives, and the student (the object) receives. The relationship tends toward the impersonal.

In pedagogical counterpoint, an I–thou relationship involves an intellectual/conversational encounter, not of subject with object but of *subject* with *subject*. The relationship is personal. Mutual presence is realized and maintained. Teacher/student presence is reciprocal. To be present to another—in Abraham Heschel's (1965, 46) words—"is to reciprocate, to offer in return for what one receives"; Ralph Harper distinguishes between "several different ways of thinking about presence ... the most acceptable [being] intimacy between persons, the miracle of giving and receiving" (Harper 1991, 4). Such reciprocity—according to William Sadler— makes it possible "to create, recognize, and reaffirm the reality of mutual presence [in which] a person [will] understand himself and be understood in terms of interpenetrating relationships with others" (Sadler 1969, 197). To achieve such an interpenetrating relationship requires that the teacher view the student as an active "subject/thou"—a *presence*—rather than as a passive "object/it." This is to understand Gabriel Marcel's recognition that "when we say that presence must not be thought of as an object, we mean the very act by which we incline ourselves toward a presence is essentially different than through which we grasp an object" (Marcel 1960, 157). To understand Marcel is to connect his awareness to Buber's definition of inclusion:

> In order to help the realization of the best potentialities of the pupil's life, the teacher must really mean him as the definite person he is in his potentiality and his actuality; more precisely, he must not know him merely as a sum of qualities, strivings, and inhibitions, he must be aware of him in his wholeness. But he can only do this if he meets him again and again as his partner in a bipolar situation .... he must practice the kind of realization which I call inclusion (*Umfassung*). (Buber 1958, 211)

All too often educators view inclusion, or inclusiveness, through a lens that narrows the focus of what this bipolar partnership should mean. When the focus is narrowed, dialogue is circumscribed and is used only as a technique to point the way to preordained conclusions. Questions are designed to lead to previously defined "correct" answers. Inclusiveness comes to represent *not* a sharing of "otherness," but rather encouraging the less powerful "other" to *join* the more powerful. In such cases, there is a diminishment of voices and identities. *Presence* is negated, and the call for inclusiveness is a "sounding gong and clashing symbol" signifying little. Such absorption of the less powerful into the "inclusiveness" of the more powerful denies the reality that:

> Inclusion is the extension of one's own concreteness, the fulfillment of the actual situation of life, the complete presence of the reality in which one participates ... This presence entails an ingathering of the other's presence ... Then there is reality *between* them, there is mutuality. (Buber 1947, 97–98)

It is this ingathering mutuality of *presence* that makes possible a democratic, inclusive learning community. As Philip Wexler has noted: "Concentrated, mindful presence is protection against the attachment of energies to a mode of dependent submission to powerful others" (Wexler 1996, 148). It takes a mutuality of teacher/student mindful presence to minimize a power/powerlessness continuum in a classroom.

In a democratic classroom, it is the teacher who is responsible for "mid-wifeing"—giving birth to—a mindful presence, for drawing forth that which is within the student. The teacher represents the helping hand. But it is the student who must provide the labor for the intellectual birth. Mixing metaphors, and paraphrasing a Taoist philosopher, "the teacher must open the door, but the student must choose to walk through it." In either case, what is necessary for a mindful/mutual presence is the disposition that John Dewey identified as the open-mindedness of "intellectual hospitality."

> Openness of mind means accessibility of mind to any and every consideration that will throw light upon the situation that needs to be cleared up ... Intellectual growth means constant expansion of horizons ... an active disposition to welcome points of view hitherto alien: an active desire to entertain considerations which modify existing purposes. Retention of capacity to grow is the reward of such intellectual hospitality. (Dewey 1916/1966, 175)

Intellectual hospitality is a disposition available to both teacher and student. It is a prerequisite for—and makes possible—a "pedagogy of presence." It allows *both* the individual "I" *and* the communal "we" to exist simultaneously. When shared intellectual hospitality is achieved in the classroom, a "we" is birthed into existence, but the "I" also remains "alive and well." There is—in the words of Albert Camus—"a 'we are' that paradoxically defines a new form of individualism ... a dignity that I cannot allow either myself or others to debase" (Camus 1957, 297). Camus's "we are" concept captures the essence of the power of *presence*. "We are" signifies not the homogeneity of a metaphorical melting pot, but rather a synthesis of thoroughly understood identities (a new form of individualism), which leads to actions that shape the good of a realistically diverse community. The individual voice is not lost in a crowd, but is part of the ever-changing rhythm of an intellectual community.

Classroom Realities: A Concluding Unscientific Postscript

This chapter has been a reflection upon an instructional philosophy in which an individually defined "pedagogy of *presence*" is presented as a methodology of choice. The definition—and the methodology—however are still in stages of refinement and represent the kind of "in-process" reflective thinking that has been spelled out by John Dewey:

> Reflective thinking involves … willingness to endure a condition of mental unrest and disturbance. Reflective thinking, in short, means judgment suspended during further inquiry; and suspense is likely to be somewhat painful … To maintain the state of doubt and to carry on systematic and protracted inquiry—these are the essentials of thinking. (Dewey 1910, 13)

To search out, and define, the foundational principles upon which a personal teaching methodology rests is a continuing process. It involves reflection on possibilities. It is a meditative, ruminative, even speculative process. There is no "now and forever" pedagogical, capital-T Truth to be translated into an absolute, immutable "best practice" in the classroom. The continuing search *is* a Deweyan "protracted inquiry."

The search is teleological, a purposeful quest. The purpose is to find the way—or perhaps more realistically *a* way—to a *real* learning community in which *presence* is revealed. Such a community provides an intellectual climate conducive for the learner—teacher and student—to seek better understanding of *both* the "self" and others through issue-oriented dialectical conversation. This is a mind-meeting-mind process requiring *I–thou* relationships. The instructional methodology is one that *educes* what the learner brings to the discussion—what s/he knows/believes and thinks/feels. But—importantly—there is another part of the educational equation. This is the *active/reflective listening*, which is part of a classroom *presence*; it requires a willingness on the part of the learner/listener to *intentionally* cultivate the ability to actively HEAR (not just listen to) what the other person is saying. It requires *reflective* thinking to counterbalance *reactive* "top-of-the-head" responses when highly charged emotional content is at issue.

Education to be meaningful must be meaning-FULL. To deal dialectically (versus ideologically) with meaningful issues, a teacher must begin with an *assumption*: "meaning" is in the eye of the beholder. And it is often hard to "hear" when a personal meaning-FULL idea, belief, or "fact" is being challenged in open dialogue. Such a challenge adds emotional struggle to the intellectual wrestling, and provides new learning opportunities. We also learn emotionally. Even the emotion of anger may lead to a significant learning experience. Reflecting upon the emotional response, we have the opportunity to ask ourselves, "why?" Why do I believe/think/act/feel—react—the way I do? If we choose to be *present* in the classroom, we will have cause to reflect on our own perceptions, presuppositions, and presumptions—even prejudices—regarding specific issues and the ideas that define the issues.

Bringing *presence* into the classroom community allows each member to develop an evolving *awareness* of the "self" and the "other" (person/idea/value, and so on). Learning occurs as I grow in awareness that my perceptions of others, and of issues, are contextual—the result of *my* experiences, *my* emotional reactions, *my* worldview, and *my* T(t)ruth. How I *hear* other people reflects the questions, concerns, priorities, intents, and goals of a unique self. But to be *educated* is to develop an increasing awareness of—and appreciation for—other unique people and ideas. I grow in self-knowledge as I am present to the other's *presence*. I can learn from the "other"—even when his/her ideas, views, and knowledge/truth are based on assumptions with which I cannot agree. *Presence* allows me to attempt to "experience" the other's ideology "from within"; for an ideology is not merely something of the head, but also of the heart, the whole being. Through the experience of mutual *presence,* there is a "mind/heart engagement," and a "*hearing/feeling*" of differing views. There is an experience of inclusion. This experienced mutuality allows each of the intellectually/emotionally engaged participants to compare and connect personal beliefs and ideas to larger meanings and purposes that transcend personal disagreements.

Here is a theory/methodology that is based on the assumption that even adult students are intellectually and emotionally "in process" as learners. There is a methodological understanding that continual learning involves questioning the "assumptions" of those with whom we disagree, but not without also critically interrogating the "whys" of our own belief system. The method is one that is centered around open-ended possibilities and question marks (?) rather than periods (.) and definitive answers; process rather than product; concepts rather than transmitted facts; and imaginative wrestling with truth(s) rather than dispensing a Truth. It allows—no, encourages—the emotions to be part of the community-of-inquiry, which is seeking to achieve an academic *koinonia* by way of a pedagogy of *presence.*

Such a community is made possible when:

1. Every "self" is affirmed and validated as a *thou* by way of a relational, interactive teaching methodology, and the student is treated not as a recipient (object) of transmitted knowledge, but as a knowledge interpreter and creator of understanding (subject).
2. Learning flows from a "pedagogical partnership" in which teacher and student *share* responsibility for the birth and development of a learning community based on a democratic process.
3. Individual differences are just not *tolerated,* but are *encouraged,* and are welcomed into the classroom dialogue.
4. The teacher balances the need for classroom structure and order with the need for student-generated issues and for student

challenges, questions, emotions, and "ways of knowing" related to "lived realities."

5. The teacher fosters an awareness and sensitivity to the numerous out-of-class influences—social, political, religious, cultural, and economic—that have a bearing on academic content and student participation.

6. The teacher *models* a concern for the personhood (dignity) of each person in the class, and places a major emphasis *not* on helping the student "to do," but on encouraging the student "to be."

A Final Postconclusion Thought

It is obvious that this is not a learning model for all situations. To invite *presence* into the classroom redefines pedagogical purpose. A pedagogy of *presence* will not satisfy the expectations of an institutional or personal educational philosophy that seeks convergent, measurable, objective, and testable outcomes. It does not fit a behaviorist model of pedagogically conditioned consistency and predictability. It does not map out a final knowledge destination. It involves risk taking for the teacher who is adventurous enough to open the class to "knowledge as a field of contending interpretations," and to the sharing of hermeneutical possibilities with students.

To bring *presence* into the classroom is to negate the absolutism of set-in-stone lesson plans, teacher-proof materials, textbook authority, and teacher hegemony. It is to stimulate—and welcome—the questions, the challenges, the intellectual skepticism that—though psychologically discomforting and pedagogically uncertain for the teacher—may make possible the existential reality of one mind penetrating another. A classroom atmosphere impregnated by *presence* encourages "zones of uncertainty" where student and teacher are challenged to critically interpret the presuppositions of both the self and the other (Slattery 1995). It is within the "zones of uncertainty"—where knowledge/truth is ambiguous and paradoxical—that strongly expressed opposing views and dynamic interchanges may shake up classroom decorum, but may also be preludes to intellectual reflection.

This kind of classroom—open to unusual insights, to new paths of awareness, and to the learning potential inherent in a cacophony of voices and divergent "ways of knowing"—requires a mutuality of *presence*. It requires the kind of inclusive mutuality that the physicist David Bohm has defined as a "participatory consciousness ... [in which] we share our consciousness and ... think together" (Bohm 1996, 23).

References

Bergkamp, V. 2000. "Laryngitis of the Soul." *Newman Review*, Spring: 6–7.
Bohm, D. 1993. *The Undivided Universe*. New York, NY: Routledge.

Bohm, D. 1996. *On Dialogue.* Edited by L. Nichol. New York, NY: Routledge.

Buber, M. 1947. *Tales of the Hasidim: The Early Masters.* New York: Schocken.

Buber, M. 1958. *I and Thou.* Translated by Ronald G. Smith. New York, NY: Scribner.

Buber, M. 1965. *Between Man and Man.* New York, NY: Collier Books.

Camus, A. 1957. *The Rebel.* New York, NY: Vintage Books.

Del Prete, T. 1990. *Thomas Merton and the Education of the Whole Person.* Birmingham, AL: Religious Education Press.

Dewey, J. 1910. *How We Think.* Mineola, NY: Dover.

Dewey, J. 1916/1966. *Democracy and Education.* New York, NY: The Free Press.

Goodlad, J., and R. Soder. 1996. *Democracy, Education, and School.* San Francisco, CA: Jossey-Bass.

Hare, W. 1998. "Critical Thinking as an Aim of Education." *Inquiry: Critical Thinking Across the Disciplines* 18 (2): 38–51.

Harper, R. 1991. *On Presence.* Philadelphia, PA: Trinity Press International.

Hazelton, R. 1960. *New Accents in Contemporary Theology.* New York: Harper.

Heschel, A. 1965. *Who Is Man?* Stanford, CA: Stanford University Press.

hooks, b., and C. West. 1991. *Breaking Bread.* Boston, MA: South End Press.

Kierkegaard, S. 1999. *Provocations: Spiritual Writings.* Edited by C. E. Moore. Farmington, PA: The Plough Publishing House.

Langbaum, R. 1982. *The Mysteries of Identity: A Theme in Modern Literature.* Chicago, IL: University of Chicago Press.

Marcel, G. 1960. *The Mystery of Being.* Chicago, IL: Henry Regnery Company.

May, R. 1976. *Power and Innocence.* New York, NY: Dell Publishing Company.

Merton, T. 1973. "Appendix III: Thomas Merton's View of Monasticism." In *The Asian Journal of Thomas Merton,* 305–308. New York, NY: New Directions Publishing.

Micallef, J. 1969. *Philosophy of Existence.* New York, NY: Philosophical Library.

Miller, R. 1982. "Theology in the Background." In *Religious Education and Theology,* edited by N. Thompson, 17–41. Birmingham, AL: Religious Education Press.

Morrison, T. 2004. *Beloved.* New York, NY: Vintage.

Pagano, J. A. 1998, February. "Presidential Address." Annual Conference, American Educational Studies Association, Philadelphia, PA.

Sadler, W. 1969. *Existence and Love.* New York, NY: Scribner.

Slattery, P. 1995. "A Postmodern Vision of Time and Learning: A Response to the National Education Commission Report *Prisoners of Time.*" *Harvard Educational Review* 65 (4): 612–633.

Sullivan, J. 1977. "The Idea of Religion—Part One." In *The Great Ideas Today,* edited by R. M. Hutchins, 204–276. Chicago, IL: Encyclopedia Britannica.

Tillich, P. 1961. *The Courage To Be.* New Haven, CT: Yale University Press.

Wexler, P. 1996. *Holy Sparks: Social Theory, Education, and Religion.* Toronto: Canadian Scholars' Press.

DON HUFFORD *is a professor of education at Newman University.*

3

Dewey (1916) described the attainment of education as a necessary tool for the establishment and sustainability of progress. Education, attending to the good of the public, is designed to instill knowledge in the constituencies it serves (Kezar 2005). Further, Woods (2004) described the design of education, its services and responsibilities, as an enterprise that promotes ethical, active engagement and respect for everyone. However, disconnects between theory and practice exist as education in the United States functions to empower some while marginalizing and oppressing others. This chapter, through a critical lens, will juxtapose ideals of equality and equity to discuss how integrating criticality and identity development into educational praxis will assist in creating inclusive, equitable practice prepared to meet the needs of learners from low socioeconomic backgrounds.

Identity, Status, and Culture: Examining Barriers of Success for Students from Low Socioeconomic Backgrounds

Anthony Walker

Introduction

The US education system has, in principle, a dual objective: to provide opportunities for all students to grow academically and to reduce inequalities in achievement and success (Konstantopoulos and Chung 2011). However, experience and research demonstrate disconnects between principles and reality. Instead, students enter the doors of education day after day, marred by the realities of inequitable resources, meager expectations, and inadequate teaching (Carlson 2008). Further, in a world defined by constructs and labels, social status is linked to ability, success, and effort.

Connections between academic success and socioeconomic status (SES) are not new to research (Phillips and Loch 2011). Highlighted by Zammit (2011), income and SES backgrounds influence teacher practice and perceptions. Also, traditional analyses highlight SES as a primary influencer in postsecondary access (Baker and Velez 1996). Preluded by

New Directions for Teaching and Learning, no. 140, Winter 2014 © 2014 Wiley Periodicals, Inc.
Published online in Wiley Online Library (wileyonlinelibrary.com) • DOI: 10.1002/tl.20110

23

negative perceptions (Zammit 2011) and inequitable access (Baker and Velez 1996), unfortunately, oftentimes labels of low SES result in students becoming disenchanted with learning due to curriculum, pedagogy, and assessment practices that reinforce messages of disconnectedness instead of engagement (Zammit 2011). And, while perceptions of higher SES often result in greater expectations from teachers (Walpole 2003), students from low SES backgrounds become acquainted with lower expectations (Auwarter and Aruguete 2008). However, at the opposite end of the spectrum lie perceptions and attitudes of inadequacy toward students from low SES backgrounds (Kappes, Oettingen, and Mayer 2012). Likewise, many times attitudes of incompetency follow the student(s) and fail to acknowledge systemic factors that contribute to students' SES. Without considerations of how SES impacts student development, perceptions, and experiences, educators fail to acknowledge that one's SES has "a significant impact on student academic performance" (Liu and Lu 2008, 71).

The Problem

Assessments such as high school GPAs and SAT scores used to evaluate intelligence and aptitude are often used to predict student persistence and ability (Smith and Wolf-Wendel 2005). Formulated to measure students' potential success, such assessments label student aptitude as innate, thus removing any link to educational and lived experiences. In turn, students become the sole shareholder of both responsibility and accountability with regard to their potential outcomes.

Data highlight subpar academic performances from students from low SES (Spencer and Castano 2007). While research demonstrates gaps in achievement between students from high and low SES backgrounds, what research often fails to highlight are subordinate levels of potential or ability. However, while research often fails to connect student potential with performance, evidence does demonstrate employments of classism as teachers "estimate their students' abilities" based on perceived social classes (Spencer and Castano 2007, 420). Thus, guided by perceptions of inadequacy and generalizations, teachers reinforce cycles of oppression as educational praxis ties ability with status. In turn, practices of education mimic the social structure that creates the stereotypes and attitudes education is theoretically designed to challenge. As primary stakeholders within the system, students fall prey to an education system inherently designed to establish standards of expectation and success through a molding of institutionalized identity development. For institutions of higher education seeking to fulfill their responsibility to the citizenry they serve, practitioners must value the uniqueness of individual identities of all students (Torres, Howard-Hamilton, and Cooper 2003).

The Solution

While research has attempted to comprehend why some students succeed and others do not, focus has remained on the role of student backgrounds (Smith and Wolf-Wendel 2005). With investigations examining how systemic structures and educational praxis influence student performance vacant from research, considerable caution is necessary when deciphering results of such an approach. Even as studies seeking to uncover reasons for achievement gaps between students from low and high SES backgrounds remain fixated in mainstream, institutionalized methods of research and practice, opportunities to initiate sustainable, progressive change do exist.

In order to establish change, acknowledgment of the problem must first be obtained. It is through such a perspective that conversations, paradigms, and assessment take root. Unsilencing the silenced, listening to rather than discrediting, and acknowledging personal biases allow educational practitioners the opportunity to gain insights into the realities of a world too often perceived through the eyes of media, perception, and privilege. However, efforts to identify systems of privilege come with great risks and responsibility when choosing paths of least resistance (Johnson 2008). For example, early on in my work with privilege, I found myself inundated with highlighting flaws in the system. Dialogue with students was, more often than not, unbalanced. By emphasizing the need to examine systemic policies and practice, values of personal accountability were often extinct from my practice and thoughts. In turn, my efforts became minimal and, at times, reinforcing of the system I sought to challenge.

Each passing day, each interaction with a student presents opportunities for growth. With personal growth comes more effective, efficient professional practice. Learning from a combination of experiential and empirical data, balance became a central component to my work. The difficulty lies less with the theory of educational practice and more with its application. An article, study, or professional development seminar is worthless without educational practitioners acknowledging the lived experiences and realities of individual students. This article, skewed to fit a solution-focused orientation, focuses less on barriers that serve as impediments to teaching and learning and more on approaches to consider while working to engage students from low SES backgrounds successfully.

Success requires certain attributes. It is of my belief that individuals from any culture are preordained to be less able, less engaged, or less successful. However, social structures built and sustained on values of power and privilege work to maintain systems of marginalization and separatism (Travis and Rosenblum 2008). Considering such realities, working with students from low SES backgrounds, as well as other disenfranchised populations, requires, as Phillips and Loch (2011) discussed, the use of approaches conducive to offsetting the negativity often connected with SES. The remainder of this chapter will examine how values of criticality and identity development may be fused with educational praxis to promote academic success.

Criticality

Explained by Kincheloe (2007), criticality considers how and why human relationships are formed in places of work, school, and throughout everyday life. An equitable, just system of education examines institutions of oppression and marginalization for the purpose of empowering all stakeholders to become engaged and have a voice. However, biased from perspectives of the dominant, too many students' voices remain silenced, questions go unasked, and dreams of what could be are smothered by realities of what is.

The installation of criticality into educational curricula is not confined to the parameters of the classroom setting. Realizing the deficiencies of curricula and practice, the role of student services has become critical in my professional practice. Working to dismantle systems of hierarchy, to challenge status quos invested in marginalization and exploitation, the value and necessity of criticality has become a priority. However, the installation of critical thinking, identity, and awareness often takes root outside of the classroom setting. Instead, difficult dialogue, critical questions of epistemology and ontology, and foci of personal connectedness between individual and systemic actions and values occur through mentorship programs, one-on-one counseling, and purposeful programming.

Identity Development

Identity reflects how one describes himself or herself within socially constructed parameters and group affiliations (Hill and Thomas 2000). In short, one's identity reflects the way they see themselves (Campbell 2010). An individual's personal identity includes attributes and commonalities shared by all human beings (Resnicow and Ross-Gaddy 1997). Although one's identity includes commonalities and attributes shared by others, the sense of self is unique to each individual.

Unique to each individual and formed amid constructs of social norms and trends, Campbell (2010) described the acclimation of identity as a process, continually changing to meet the needs of both the individual and society. It is imperative that practitioners acknowledge identity development, a process of lifelong learning and individual growth, for its uniqueness from student to student and not engage in practice that simplifies identity to generalizable, group-based assumptions and statements (Torres, Howard-Hamilton, and Cooper 2003).

Efforts to establish practices focused on the identity development of students are comprehensive. As DeMars and Erwin (2004) discussed, identity development involves more than the learning involved in any particular course; instead, the process encompasses the students' entire university experience. For educational practitioners, the process of developing students' identities begins with themselves. Noted by Travis and Rosenblum (2008), fundamental to the change process is the discovery of the authentic self and recognizing the multifaceted, constantly evolving sense of identity—and then making sure methods of practice are consistent with that identity of self. Educational praxis intent on invoking values of lifelong learning into the processes of identity development values both similarities and differences involved in deconstructing one's identity (Torres, Howard-Hamilton, and Cooper 2003). Further, such practice requires practitioners to appreciate the processes students must engage in to gain a greater sense of self and identity.

Example of Practice

With nearly 10 years of experience in higher education, I have had ample amounts of experience working with students from a multitude of SES backgrounds. In particular, I worked at one institution whose student body consisted primarily of students from low SES backgrounds. Working at an institution in which more than 90 percent of the student population was Pell Grant eligible, I have been afforded the opportunity to work with students whose intelligence and potential have been labeled as insufficient due to physical attributes and social constructs, rather than ability and aptitude. Believing in the responsibilities of education (Konstantopoulos and Chung 2011), and knowing disconnects between theory and practice of education, identity development has become a focal point of my work with students.

Sadly, too many conversations equating success to simply getting to college, completing the first year, or living to see the age of 20 are implanted into my memory and psyche. Testimonies of being "just a poor kid coming from nothing, trying to make it," or "the first in my family to attend college" have filled my office too many times. While to some such statements might appear to be nothing more than statements coming from a student's mouth, for me they are demonstrations of a broken, unjust education system. And, more importantly, such statements represent an acknowledgment of responsibility, a desire to succeed, as well as feelings of doubt, inadequacy, and worry.

It was during my second year of working at a small, rural, liberal arts college that I met a young man whose testimonies of life and yearnings for more demonstrated the power of criticality, awareness, and identity development. The young man's, Greg (pseudonym), lived experiences and personal testimonies reflected an upbringing of living just above the poverty line, moving from apartment to apartment, and navigating an education system focused less on teaching and learning and more on crowd control and survival.

Greg, now a junior in college, was the product of a disengaged, uncritical, and unjust education system. His conversations reflected a young man filled with curiosity, questions, and passion. However, his experiences had silenced him. Expectations of subpar intelligence, incongruence between educational curricula and lived reality, and associations between background and ability thwarted Greg's desire to engage with teachers and the classroom. Instead, Greg, like many of his peers, became a victim of a broken educational system, a system failing to fulfill what Konstantopoulos and Chung (2011) described as a fundamental responsibility to educate all students.

Empathizing with their dejectedness and frustrations, I had an open door policy that welcomed Greg and other students into my office. What initially began as nothing more than pass-by visits to say hello and check in quickly became meetings filled with opportunities to engage and empower Greg. Our dialogue reflected questions of criticality as Greg's curiosity was reignited. Focused on empowering Greg, my work consisted of listening first, speaking second. Removing the muzzles that had for far too long stifled his voice, Greg's experiences became the platform for both my and his teaching and learning. Every experience, every reality offered an opportunity to challenge Greg, to develop his identity, and to connect learning with both education and life.

Week after week, day after day, Greg's growth became more and more apparent. What was once a young man whose actions reflected practices of a system of standardization, Greg learned how to situate himself, his teachings and experiences, within the institutionalisms of the greater system. Now engaged in a lifelong process, Greg had become more than a student, he was a learner.

Conclusion

I have often been asked questions prefixed with how and why. How do I engage students from diverse backgrounds whose experiences are filled with disenfranchisement and marginalization? Why do students, often from cultural backgrounds and lived realities far different from my own, interact, open up, and allow themselves to be vulnerable with me? For me, that answer lies less in the balancing of theory with practice.

A fundamental component to student growth is the idea that one's college years are vital to the development of identity (Torres, Howard-Hamilton, and Cooper 2003). Invested in values of critical theory, and acknowledging connections between college and identity development, I seek to empower students. My intent is to create a learning environment of challenges and questions that promote criticality, awareness, and identity development. Working with students from low SES backgrounds requires much responsibility, attention, and effort. However, these efforts are required when working with all students, regardless of their background. A fundamental difference lies less in the practice of pedagogies and more in the critique and challenging of self on behalf of the practitioner. As reported by Torres, Howard-Hamilton, and Cooper (2003), knowledge and understanding of one's own identity is a precursor to truly recognizing another individual's culture.

Examining personal biases, critiquing the filters of knowledge and information that guide learning and values, and instituting criticality into practice are steps in the right direction. While the responsibility to education is institutional, situational, and unique to each student (Smith and Wolf-Wendel 2005), the empowerment of students begins with practitioners. Students cannot be expected to value criticality, to be aware, and to know who they are if practitioners (1) fail to encourage such explorations; (2) do not institute practice that promotes critical thinking, awareness, and identity development; (3) are not critical and aware of themselves; and (4) are unable to answer questions of who they are or how and why they became the person they are. The responsibility of education is to all (Konstantopoulos and Chung 2011), including those from low SES backgrounds. At the core of a just and equitable education, inclusive in the engagement and learning is practice that encourages criticality, awareness, and identity development of all students.

References

Auwarter, A. E., and M. S. Aruguete. 2008. "Effects of Student Gender and Socioeconomic Status on Teacher Perceptions." *The Journal of Educational Research* 101 (4): 242–246.

Baker, T. L., and W. Velez. 1996. "Access to and Opportunity in Postsecondary Education in the United States: A Review." *Sociology of Education* 69 (2): 82–101.

Campbell, D. E. 2010. *Choosing Democracy: A Practical Guide to Multicultural Education*, 4th ed. Boston, MA: Pearson Education.

Carlson, D. 2008. "Are We Making Progress? The Discursive Construction of Progress in the Age of No Child Left Behind." In *Keeping the Promise: Essays on Leadership, Democracy, and Education*, edited by D. Carlson and C. P. Gause, Vol. 306, 3–26. New York, NY: Peter Lang.

DeMars, C. E., and T. D. Erwin. 2004. "Scoring Neutral or Unsure on an Identity Development for Higher Education. *Research in Higher Education* 45 (1): 83–95.

Dewey, J. 1916. *Democracy in Education: An Introduction to the Philosophy of Education*. New York, NY: The Free Press.

Hill, M. R., and V. Thomas. 2000. "Strategies for Racial Identity Development Narratives of Black and White Women in Interracial Partner Relationships." *Family Relations* 49 (2): 193–200.

Johnson, A. G. 2008. "What Can We Do: Becoming Part of the Solution." In *The Meaning of Difference: American Constructions of Race, Sex and Gender, Social Class, Sexual Orientation, and Disability*, edited by K. Rosenblum and T. C. Travis, 5th ed., 502–507. Boston, MA: McGraw-Hill College.

Kappes, H. B., G. Oettingen, and D. Mayer. 2012. "Positive Fantasies Predict Low Academic Achievement in Disadvantaged Students." *European Journal of Social Psychology* 42 (1): 53–64.

Kezar, A. J. 2005. "Challenges for Higher Education in Serving the Public Good." In *Higher Education for the Public Good: Emerging Voices from a National Movement*, edited by A. J. Kezar, T. C. Chambers, J. C. Burkhardt, and Associates, 23–42. San Francisco, CA: Jossey-Bass.

Kincheloe, J. L. 2007. "Postformalism and Critical Multiculturalism: Educational Psychology and the Power of Multilogicality." In *The Praeger Handook of Education and Psychology*, edited by J. L. Kincheloe and R. A. Horn, Jr., Vol. 4, 876–898. Westport, CT: Praeger.

Konstantopoulos, S., and V. Chung. 2011. "Teacher Effects on Minority and Disadvantaged Students' Grade 4 Achievement." *The Journal of Educational Research* 104 (2): 73–86.

Liu, X., and K. Lu. 2008. "Student Performance and Family Socioeconomic Status: Results from a Survey of Compulsory Education in Western China." *Chinese Education and Society* 41 (5): 70–83.

Phillips, P., and B. Loch. 2011. "Building Lectures and Building Bridges with Socio-Economically Disadvantaged Students." *Educational Technology and Society* 14 (3): 240–251.

Resnicow, K., and D. Ross-Gaddy. 1997. "Development of a Racial Identity Scale for Low Income African Americans." *Journal of Black Studies* 28 (2): 239–254.

Smith, D. G., and L. E. Wolf-Wendel. 2005. "The Role of Student Characteristics." In *ASHE Higher Education Report: The Challenge of Diversity: Involvement or Alienation in the Academy?*, Vol. 31, No. 1, 21–24. San Francisco, CA: Jossey-Bass.

Spencer, B., and E. Castano. 2007. "Social Class Is Dead. Long Live Social Class! Stereotype Threat among Low Socioeconomic Status Individuals." *Social Justice Research* 20 (4): 418–432.

Torres, V., M. F. Howard-Hamilton, and D. L. Cooper. 2003. "Why Should Higher Education Be Concerned with the Identity Development of Diverse Students." In *ASHE Higher Education Report: Identity Development of Diverse Populations: Implications for Teaching and Administration in Higher Education*, Vol. 29, No. 6, 1–8. San Francisco, CA: Jossey-Bass.

Travis, T.-M., and K. Rosenblum. 2008. "Framework Essay." In *The Meaning of Difference: American Constructions of Race, Sex and Gender, Social Class, Sexual Orientation, and Disability*, edited by K. E. Travis and T. C. Rosenblum, 5th ed., 334–350. Boston, MA: McGraw-Hill College.

Walpole, M. B. 2003. "Socioeconomic Status and College: How SES Affects College Experiences and Outcomes." *The Review of Higher Education* 27 (1): 45–73.

Woods, P. A. 2004. "Democratic Leadership: Drawing Distinctions with Distributed Leadership." *International Journal of Leadership in Education* 7 (1): 3–26.

Zammit, K. P. 2011. "Connecting Multiliteracies and Engagement of Students from Low Socio-Economic Backgrounds: Using Bernstein's Pedagogy Discourse as a Bridge." *Language and Education* 25 (3): 203–220.

ANTHONY WALKER *is the director of Student Success and Completion at Tarrant County College and an adjunct professor at Texas Christian University.*

4

Racial awareness is a critical foundation to racial sensitivity, and it is a necessity for future professionals who want to be prepared to succeed in an increasingly diverse society. Several factors have been shown to influence racial awareness in professionals including their own race, their personal experience with racism, and the amount/quality of training they receive on the topic of race. Institutions of higher education that pride themselves on preparing students to work in a global and diverse market should make a purposeful effort to teach students how to address issues related to race and racism. This chapter offers recommendations for how to transform traditional programs into programs with a focus on antiracism using a Critical Race Theory paradigm. For example, curricula should be designed to challenge students to focus on their personal experiences of racism and racial identity rather than simply studying others'. Student resistance can be minimized by recruiting faculty and students with not only racial diversity, but with diversity of experiences with racism. Finally, by purposefully engaging in interdisciplinary work on campus, smaller departments or more homogeneous departments can provide racial minority students with much needed opportunities for racial identity development and cross-racial interactions.

Addressing Racial Awareness and Color-Blindness in Higher Education

Kimberly Diggles

Institutions of higher education that pride themselves on training future professionals prepared to work and succeed in an increasingly diverse society should make a purposeful effort to teach students how to address issues related to race and racism. It may be tempting to believe that race and racism are no longer the important issues they were two generations ago and that American society has finally moved beyond the racial atrocities of the past. However, race and racism are still current issues with implications for several facets of people's lives. In 1997, the American Psychological Association acknowledged that racial prejudices continue to exist and that race and skin color still "figure prominently in everyday attitudes" (2).

New Directions for Teaching and Learning, no. 140, Winter 2014 © 2014 Wiley Periodicals, Inc.
Published online in Wiley Online Library (wileyonlinelibrary.com) • DOI: 10.1002/tl.20111

This claim has been supported by several empirical studies in which most participants, even racial minorities, had implicit, automatic positive associations with White people and automatic negative associations with people they identified as racial minorities (Burston, Jones, and Robertson-Saunders 1995; Correll et al. 2002; Eisenberg and Johnson 2004; Feagin 2006; Nosek, Banaji, and Greenwald 2002).

Racial minorities, compared to Whites, also face overt acts of racism in several life domains pertinent to their ability to achieve success. For example, several studies that examined racism in the job market consistently found that despite progress in employment laws and policies, employers often chose to not hire candidates belonging to racial minority groups, especially when White candidates of equal (or sometimes lesser) qualification were available (Bertrand and Mullainathan 2004; Blumrosen and Blumrosen 1999; Pager and Western 2004). In the domain of education, research also found that students attending predominately minority schools are less likely to have high-quality and experienced teachers or college-preparatory classes (Clotfelter, Ladd, and Vigdor 2005; Grant-Thomas 2010; Hanushek, Kain, and Rivkin 2004; Jackson 2009). Besides having a direct effect on racial minorities' propensity for success and achievement, racism has a negative effect on psychological well-being. Undoubtedly, being treated unfairly for any reason could have an adverse effect on any person's psyche. However, racial discrimination is considered to be an especially detrimental type of unjust treatment due to the marginalized status of racial minorities within society (Williams and Williams-Morris 2000).

Because of the continued adverse consequences of explicit and implicit racism, sensitivity to these issues is required of faculty and staff who work with racial minorities. Likewise, if institutions wish to train future professionals who can compete in a diverse society, these institutions must make racial sensitivity a primary part of the curriculum. A critical foundation to racial sensitivity is *racial awareness*, a person's "ability to recognize that race exists and that it shapes reality in inequitable and unjust ways" (Laszloffy and Hardy 2000, 36).

Racial Awareness and Color-Blindness

To be racially aware is to acknowledge the fact that real life is not always just or that society does not always offer merit-based rewards to people of all races (Neville et al. 2000). Those with racial awareness can begin to address issues of racism because they have a cognitive understanding of the continued existence of race-based privilege and oppression.

Neville et al. (2000) have highlighted that those without this awareness often deny or minimize the continued influence of race on reality. Such a worldview is known as *color-blindness* (Neville et al. 2000). Color-blind attitudes, even as they exist in the most well-intentioned of people, ignore the fact that (1) certain laws and policies continue to imply White superiority over racial minorities, (2) privileges are afforded to people belonging to the White race that inherently place racial minorities at certain disadvantages, and (3) general race-based discrimination continues to pervade the daily lives of racial minorities (Neville et al. 2000). Color-blindness is often seen in the ideals of *postracial liberalism*: a combination of rhetoric that transcends race and the push of race-neutral policy agendas based on the assumption that racism is no longer an influential factor for disparities between the races (Wise 2010).

Color-blind ideologies may stem from a distorted belief that openly claiming to see skin color and race as a significant factor that shapes reality makes one racist (Hardy and Laszloffy 2008). In a study of private versus public self-reports of racial attitudes, Plant and Devine (1998) found that college students were highly motivated by fear of social disapproval to appear racially neutral even if this was not their authentic stance. Findings by Bonilla-Silva (2006) also suggested that some people, especially Whites, are more likely to speak in cautious "double-talk," "beat around the bush," or use politically correct semantics when discussing race so as not to mistakenly appear racist (164). Hardy and Laszloffy (2008) however take great care in pointing out that acknowledging the influence of race on present-day society and discussing such issues candidly are not the same as racial discrimination or being racist.

Negative Effects of Color-Blindness.   Denying the continuing influence of race does not effectively make racism less of a reality. Instead, color-blind attitudes expressed by persons of any race support the perpetuation of racist ideologies in several ways (Hardy and Laszloffy 2008; Neville et al. 2000; Sue et al. 2007). First, the minimization of racism or the blatant denial of individual racial biases has been identified as a type of racial microaggression (Sue et al. 2007). Secondly, those with color-blind attitudes will be less likely to take action against modern-day systemic oppression of racial minorities because they do not acknowledge or cannot recognize that it even exists, thereby supporting proracist ideologies by tolerating the status quo (Frankenberg 1993).

Color-blindness also perpetuates racist ideologies by denying the system of privilege and oppression that exists on the basis of race. When this system is ignored or minimized, the disparities that exist between racial minorities and Whites are erroneously attributed to the shortcomings of those minorities. As a result, solutions are then aimed solely at fixing those perceived shortcomings, and the results are ineffective (Bonilla-Silva 2006; Frankenberg 1993; Wise 2008).

For example, Bill Cosby (2004) demonstrated his own color-blindness when he used postracial ideologies to repeatedly blame the plight of the Black community on a supposed lack of family values and moral standing:

> Today, ladies and gentlemen, in our cities and public schools we have fifty percent drop out. In our own neighborhoods, we have men in prison. No

longer is a person embarrassed because they're pregnant without a husband. No longer is a boy considered an embarrassment if he tries to run away from being the father of the unmarried child. (paragraph 2)

Even more recently, President Barack Obama (2006) wrote, "...what ails the working-class and middle-class Blacks and Latinos is not fundamentally different from what ails their White counterparts..." (245). Comments such as President Obama's and Bill Cosby's minimize or ignore the roles of historical oppression and current institutional discrimination in the cause and maintenance of racial inequities. This denial prevents policy makers from targeting the root causes of racial inequity and runs the risk of placing blame on racial minorities for social problems.

When people working to provide services to racial minorities (that is, student services professionals, mental health clinicians, and professors) deny that they harbor racial biases, they fail to recognize their position of power relative to that of their clients or students. The color-blind person also minimizes the racial experiences of those they work with, therefore jeopardizing engagement and retention (Casmir and Morrison 1993; Sue et al. 2007). If future professionals are going to be able to enter their respective fields and be successfully able to collaborate with stakeholders and engage consumers, they will need an education that teaches them to be aware of modern-day racial realities.

Influences on Racial Awareness.   Several factors have been shown to influence racial awareness including race, personal experience with racism, and cultural competency training.

Race and Racial Awareness.   The role of race in the development of racial awareness may be a function of people's general resistance to acknowledging their social positions of privilege, and their privileged experiences also ensure the ongoing oppression of those outside of their group (Gushue and Constantine 2007; Neville et al. 2001). On the other hand, people are much more willing and able to recognize the ways in which their social positions cause them to be oppressed and marginalized. This means that White Americans are more likely to lack awareness of their racial privilege and the ways in which the benefits they so often enjoy maintain the gaps between themselves and minorities (Advisory Board to the President's Initiative on Race 1998). Racial minorities, on the other hand, are likely to be quite aware of the social ramifications of being a racial minority in America (Bonilla-Silva 2006; Helm, Sedlacek, and Prieto 1998; Jackson 1999; Laszloffy and Hardy 2000; Worthington et al. 2008). When racial minorities are unaware of the racial realities around them, they risk violating implicit social codes regarding acceptable cross-race interactions, the results of which can potentially be severe. Helm, Sedlacek, and Prieto (1998) articulated this difference of reality between Whites and racial minorities: "It is likely that Whites do not see the relevance of their culture to diversity issues because the overall culture . . . has been, and continues to be, designed for them" (115). Likewise, Laszloffy and Hardy (2000) reported that racial minorities, relative to Whites, are more racially aware because they are socialized from an early age to recognize how to navigate racial interactions in such a way that protects them from racially motivated dangers and leaves Whites feeling comfortable in their presence. On the other hand, White Americans are actually more likely to promote ideas of racial unawareness when teaching their children about race relations (Hamm 2001). One example of this might be a well-intentioned White mother who tells her young son that he should not bring attention to the fact that his new friend is Asian because he should not "see color."

Most of the literature that has explicitly examined racial awareness and color-blind attitudes in racial minorities either has been limited to samples solely consisting of Black Americans or does not have large enough samples of other minority groups to allow for a meaningful analysis. However, there has been some evidence that indicates that racial awareness may appear differently across various minority groups. For example, a 2001 survey sponsored by the Kaiser Foundation suggested that although Hispanic and Asian Americans were less likely than Whites to endorse color-blind beliefs, they were more likely than Black Americans to agree with statements consistent with color-blind ideologies (Washington Post, Kaiser Family Foundation, Harvard University 2011).

Black parents were also found to be significantly more likely than Mexican and Japanese-American parents to transmit messages regarding racism and discrimination to their children (Phinney and Chavira 1995), thus demonstrating that Black parents have an acute awareness of the realities of racism. Also, the children who received these messages from their parents were more likely than children who did not receive these messages to also show increases in racial awareness (Phinney and Chavira 1995).

Personal Experience with Racism and Racial Awareness.   The link between personal experiences with racial discrimination and racial awareness is an intuitive one. Individuals who have reported experiencing personal injustices based on their race are probably more likely to be aware of overall cultural and institutional climates, which often determine rewards based on skin color. In their study of influencing variables on perceptions of racial–ethnic climates, for example, Worthington et al. (2008) found that participants who experienced their college campus as having a negative climate toward racial minorities also tended to have higher levels of racial awareness. Also, parents were more likely to demonstrate and promote racially aware messages to their children when the family had experienced racism (Hughes 2003; Hughes and Chen 1997; Stevenson et al. 2002, 2005).

As mentioned earlier, racial minorities are less likely than Whites to endorse color-blind racial attitudes. This influence of race on racial awareness appears to be, at least in part, a function of personal experiences of racism as racial minorities are more likely than Whites to experience racial discrimination and more likely to perceive themselves as the direct targets of racism.

However, just as all minority groups do not display the same levels of racial awareness, they also do not perceive or experience racism in the same way. Although Latino students were more likely to report feeling strong pressure to conform to racial stereotypes than White students, they were less likely than Black and Asian students to endorse these realities (Ancis, Sedlacek, and Mohr 2000). Blacks were found to be more likely than other minority groups to report experiencing daily microaggressions or racial conflict (Ancis, Sedlacek, and Mohr 2000; Mont-Reynaud, Ritter, and Chen 1990). These findings may provide some explanation for why Black parents provide their children with more racial awareness messages than other minority groups (Biafora et al. 1993; Hughes 2003; Hughes and Chen 1999; Phinney and Chavira 1995).

It should be noted that vicarious racism—witnessing or hearing about another person's or group's experience with racial discrimination—"can also teach valuable lessons about the places where racism hides and resides" (Harrell 2000, 45) and, therefore, is a more accessible avenue through which Whites can experience the existence of racial discrimination and increase their awareness of the realities of racism within society without having to be a direct victim of the experience.

Education and Racial Awareness. Rather than being due to blatant racism or explicit beliefs in White superiority, lack of racial awareness is often due to a lack of knowledge and can likely be combated with education and training. Racial awareness in higher education is usually sought in conjunction with overall cultural competency, which has been defined as improving students' ability to "integrate issues of diversity into their work" (Vera and Speight 2003, 253).

Many institutions and curricula within higher education choose to utilize a traditional model of cultural competency training that tends to focus on skills-based competencies and the process of identifying personal biases. This traditional paradigm has been heavily criticized as being too focused on individual attitudes, therefore leaving students and future professionals "unequipped to deal with institutional racism and oppression on all of the levels where it permeates" (Abrams and Moio 2006, 247). In other words, traditional cultural competency paradigms neglect to deeply expose students to ways in which oppression and privilege affect marginalized groups across several systems of society.

Another criticism of traditional cultural competence training has been that current teaching paradigms often lack specific and concrete objectives related to racial justice. Rather, discussions of oppression and privilege have been expanded in order to simultaneously focus on several categories of social difference (Abrams and Moio 2006). For example, in an article describing a mental health multicultural competency course, topics included:

> culture, White privilege, race, racism, oppression, social class, cultural iden-
> tity/genogram, gender, self-of-the-therapist, child-free couples, voluntary
> single-parenthood, adoption, gay/lesbian families, families of African origin,
> Asian families, Hispanic families, Middle-Eastern families, families of Euro-
> pean descent, Immigrant families, Jewish families, religion/spirituality, and
> disabilities. (Murphy, Park, and Lonsdale 2006, 307)

Students in the Murphy, Park, and Lonsdale (2006) study demonstrated increases in their multicultural knowledge immediately following
the end of the course. However, it was unclear as to whether or not these
increases were long term or if their awareness of racial justice issues specif-
ically was changed.

Although the expansion of cultural competency curriculum to include
as many forms of oppression as possible has been an expected and honor-
able response to academia's realization that people have multiple identities,
it also prevents an in-depth analysis of any one type of oppression or social construct. Even more dangerous, this pedagogy assumes an equality-
of-oppressions stance that places content relevant to racial minorities at
risk of being overshadowed or diminished all together while reinforcing the
idea that racism does not exist or currently affect individuals and families
(Schiele 2007). When interviewed about their experiences of racism within
their graduate programs, students of color often reported feeling oppressed
when a lack of attention was paid to racial issues (McDowell 2004).

Critical Race Theory Paradigm of Cultural Competency Training

Discussions of more effective methods of delivering racial competence
training within higher education have already begun within the field of
social work education using the framework of critical race theory (CRT).
CRT, as described by Delgado and Stefancic (2001), has several tenets: (1)
though a social construct, race has forceful meaning and real implications,
especially for racial minorities, (2) racism is oftentimes so commonplace
and pervasive within the fabric of society that it is frequently invisible, and
(3) this invisibility is also what helps to maintain its existence. Critics of traditional cultural competency teaching paradigms have suggested that curriculum should move from a pedagogy of antioppression—"a term loosely
applied to models that identify exclusion and oppression from within and
outside of the profession"—to one of antiracism—similar to antioppression,
except it "positions race as a central mechanism of oppression" (Abrams and
Moio 2006, 253). Antiracist frameworks assume the following: (1) race has
salient social effects despite the lack of biological basis for the concept of

race, (2) historical processes of White power continue to exist as a reservoir of privilege for White Americans, (3) the role of traditional institutions is to produce and maintain race-based inequalities, and (4) the problems of racial minorities cannot be understood out of context from the "ideological circumstances in which minorities find themselves" (Maiter 2009, 270).

Suggestions for Implementation.   By teaching and supervising from a CRT framework, institutions can help students develop skills to reframe individual racism from a critically conscious lens, which can then be generalized to other types of social oppression. In this way "race remains central and does not get lost" (Abrams and Moio 2006, 255). Three of the biggest obstacles to taking an antiracist approach are: (1) providing effective experiences in a classroom setting, (2) overcoming student resistance, and (3) ensuring that instructors are prepared to teach CRT content.

Providing Effective Experiences.   There has been a general consensus in the literature that in order to be effective in increasing racial awareness, educational experiences ought to be experiential and transformative in nature. These experiences should also be weaved throughout students' entire campus experience and higher education curriculum rather than single classes or optional coursework.

The use of books, movies, and other publications that overtly illustrate racial experiences are effective ways in which instructors can introduce students to racism and privilege within the context of the classroom (McDowell et al. 2002; McGoldrick et al. 1999), although adding these things alone may hinder the advanced development of racial consciousness (Zimmerman and Haddock 2001). For students who are beyond the early stages of racial awareness, less overt examples can be used to illustrate more subtle instances of racism and privilege as well as encourage students to use a critical antiracist framework to critique traditional theories (McDowell and Shelton 2002; McDowell et al. 2002; McGeorge et al. 2006; Zimmerman and Haddock 2001).

Also, requiring students to participate in out-of-class cross-racial events can give them firsthand racial experiences that they may otherwise not receive in their personal lives (Laszloffy and Hardy 2000). These types of experiences increase the chances for organic cross-racial interaction between students, which is a much more effective way to increase consciousness rather than artificial or secondhand experiences (McDowell et al. 2002).

Campus programming and classroom discussions should purposefully challenge students to engage in active consideration of race—their own as well as that of others. Pushing students to focus on their personal experiences of racism and racial identity is cited as being an important component to developing racial awareness (McDowell and Shelton 2002; McGoldrick et al. 1999). This type of identity work helps students become aware of their own roles in the system of race-based privilege and oppression, thus deepening their awareness of how race shapes reality (Laszloffy and Hardy 2000).

Reducing Student Resistance.   Discussing one's own role in systemic oppression and privilege can be difficult; feelings of guilt and resistance are often normal during the process of becoming more racially aware (Abrams and Moio 2006). Challenges with student resistance can be minimized, however, if institutions reconsider their methods for increasing racial diversity within their student bodies and faculty. The most common strategy taken by institutions for attempting to create environments conducive to the facilitation of meaningful interactions around issues of race is to increase compositional diversity (Milem, Chang, and Antonio 2005). This strategy has also even been suggested in the literature as a strategy for providing students with more frequent and more organic experiences with race (McGeorge et al. 2006; McGoldrick et al. 1999). Although it can enhance diversity, using this tactic alone runs the risk of actually perpetuating the proracist ideology that only racial minorities care about advocating for racial justice and further isolating racial minorities who begin to be viewed as tokens of "diversity with whom all others should interact" (Milem, Chang, and Antonio 2005, 19). Milem, Chang, and Antonio (2005) also added that utilizing this method alone causes leaders to lose sight of the fact that racial diversity is "an educational process" serving to increase racial competency outcomes rather than "an end in itself" (16).

Leaders of individual programs should also focus on recruiting and admitting students who will not only add to the compositional diversity of their programs, but who can also demonstrate an understanding of why antiracism is paramount to competent practice and research. Programs should purposefully recruit students who are able to identify personal experiences they have had with issues related to racism—direct or vicarious—and can articulate the effect these experiences have had on their development. These students can easily be identified during their application or interview process. These experiences, rather than race alone, are more demonstrative of students' awareness of social realities and perhaps their openness to bringing issues of racism (and other types of oppression) into discussions of their personal and professional development. Furthermore, programs and campuses that struggle to recruit racial minorities, intentionally looking more broadly for students with personal experiences with racism, can help ensure that their programs have learners who recognize the importance of racial justice and can contribute to more meaningful interactions even if they are not racial minorities themselves.

Ensuring Instructor Preparedness.   In order to address the third challenge associated with taking an antiracist approach to cultural competency training and instructor preparedness, individual programs within an institution should be willing to acknowledge when they are limited by the size or expertise of their faculty and unable to provide students with comprehensive, multidimensional antiracism socialization. In such cases, regular and unambiguous interdisciplinary collaboration with other on-campus programs and departments with more CRT expertise (that is, cultural studies and public policy) can be a first step toward addressing such limitations. Such practice would not only provide students with access to faculty members who specialize in antiracist models of teaching cultural competence, but it would also publicly model a willingness to engage in cross-group interactions at a systems level. Such collaborations could take several forms including interdisciplinary faculty research projects on which students take assistantship positions, students taking courses taught within these other departments, regularly inviting lecturers from other departments to cofacilitate classes, and regular research symposiums during which research on issues of race and racism are presented and the findings discussed in a seminar format.

Even if interdisciplinary collaboration is implemented, programs with limited racial expertise should also have goals to recruit more faculty members from their field who are doing research on issues related to race, faculty members who are experienced and trained in CRT pedagogy, and faculty members who demonstrate competency in facilitating dialogue about institutional racism in and outside of the classroom. Although Abrams and Moio (2006) suggested that racial minority faculty and junior-level faculty are more likely to fit these criteria, the same caution should be taken in recruiting faculty as was suggested when recruiting students. Assuming that all non-White faculty members are comfortable and competent in delivering effective antiracism pedagogy is not necessarily accurate. Assuming that non-White faculty members are the only ones who are able to discuss difficult issues pertaining to race also runs the risk of turning them into tokens, which further perpetuates proracist ideologies and also risks missing out on White faculty who have the experiences and training to facilitate a great paradigm shift.

Creating an Antiracist Environment.   Besides providing access to racial experts and mentors, interdisciplinary collaboration and better recruitment of faculty will start to transform the campuses and classrooms in which students and future professionals learn. One characteristic of university campuses that specialize in antiracist issues is that like-minded participants who, along with the faculty and staff, contribute to rich discussions and interactions about antiracist ideals also usually attend them. Phelan et al. (1995) endorsed the supposition that students' attitudes and ideologies are influenced by their educational environments where the "ideal culture is transmitted" (130). Students who are able to find themselves immersed in environments and consistent interactions where the "ideal culture" is one that prioritizes antiracism are more likely to be socialized toward that way of thinking than those who are not. Conversely, students who do not venture out into these arenas are likely being socialized toward an "ideal culture" where the status quo ideologies of color-blindness are perpetuated.

Although students' direct engagement in opportunities provided by the changes that have been suggested would vary due to individual student characteristics, Milem, Chang, and Antonio (2005) suggested that simply being in an environment committed to antiracism can impact students' attitudes and beliefs. Furthermore, such a demonstration of commitment to racial justice would help ensure that racial minorities recruited onto predominately White campuses are not considered tokens for racial diversity, but rather are also seen as being potential beneficiaries of antiracist initiatives. Racial minority students also need opportunities for racial identity development and cross-racial interactions.

References

Abrams, L. S., and J. A. Moio. 2006. "Critical Race Theory and the Cultural Competence Dilemma in Social Work Education." *Journal of Social Work Education* 45 (2): 245–261.

Advisory Board to the President's Initiative on Race. 1998. *One America in the 21st Century: Forging a New Future.* Washington, DC: U.S. Government Printing Office. Accessed March 15, 2012. https://www.ncjrs.gov/txtfiles/173431.txt.

American Psychological Association. 1997. *Can—or Should—America Be Color-Blind? Psychological Research Reveals Fallacies in Color-Blind Response to Racism* [Pamphlet]. Washington, DC: Author.

Ancis, J. R., W. E. Sedlacek, and J. J. Mohr. 2000. "Student Perceptions of Campus Cultural Climate by Race." *Journal of Counseling and Development* 78 (2): 180–185.

Bertrand, M., and S. Mullainathan. 2004. "Are Emily and Greg More Employable Than Lakisha and Jamal? A Field Experiment in Labor Market Discrimination." *The American Economic Review* 94 (4): 991–1013.

Biafora, F. A., G. J. Warheit, R. S. Zimmerman, and A. G. Gil. 1993. "Racial Mistrust and Deviant Behaviors among Ethnically Diverse Black Adolescent Boys." *Journal of Applied Social Psychology* 23: 891–910.

Blumrosen, A., and R. Blumrosen. 1999. *The Reality of Intentional Job Discrimination in Metropolitan American: 1999.* Newark, NJ: Rutgers University. http://www.rci.rutgers.edu/~nwklaw/blumrosen/Title.pdf.

Bonilla-Silva, E. 2006. *Racism without Racists: Color-Blind Racism and the Persistence of Racial Inequality in the United States,* 2nd ed. Lanham, MD: Rowman & Littlefield Publishers.

Burston, B. W., D. Jones, and P. Robertson-Saunders. 1995. "Drug Use and African Americans: Myth Versus Reality." *Journal of Alcohol and Drug Education* 40 (2): 19–35.

Casmir, G. J., and B. J. Morrison. 1993. "Rethinking Work with 'Multicultural Populations.' " *Community Mental Health Journal* 29 (6): 547–559.

Clotfelter, C. T., H. F. Ladd, and J. Vigdor. 2005. "Who Teaches Whom? Race and the Distribution of Novice Teachers." *Economics Education Review* 24 (2): 377–392.

Correll, J., B. Park, C. M. Judd, and B. Wittenbrink. 2002. "The Police Officer's Dilemma: Using Ethnicity to Disambiguate Potentially Threatening Individuals." *Journal of Personality and Social Psychology* 83 (6): 1314–1329.

Cosby, B. 2004. "50th Anniversary Commemoration of the Brown vs. Topeka Board of Education Supreme Court Decision Keynote Address." Presented at the NAACP Awards Ceremony, Washington, DC. Accessed February 6, 2012. http://www.eightcitiesmap.com/transcript_bc.htm.

Delgado, R., and J. Stefancic. 2001. *Critical Race Theory: An Introduction.* New York, NY: New York University.

Eisenberg, T., and S. L. Johnson. 2004. "Implicit Racial Attitudes of Death Penalty Lawyers." *DePaul Law Review* 53: 1539–1556.

Feagin, J. R. 2006. *Systemic Racism: A Theory of Oppression.* New York, NY: Routledge.

Frankenberg, R. 1993. *White Women, Race Maters: The Social Construction of Whiteness.* Minneapolis, MN: University of Minnesota Press.

Grant-Thomas, A. 2010. "Accusing Someone of Racism Squashes the Likelihood of Fruitful Dialogue Like a Bug." *Huffington Post.* Accessed March 10, 2012. http://www .huffingtonpost.com/andrew-grantthomas-phd/accusing-someone-of-racis_b_414743 .html.

Gushue, G. V., and M. G. Constantine. 2007. "Color-Blind Racial Attitudes and White Racial Identity Attitudes in Psychology Trainees." *Professional Psychology: Research and Practice* 38 (3): 321–328.

Hamm, J. V. 2001. "Barriers and Bridges to Positive Cross-Ethnic Relations: African American and White Parent Socialization Beliefs and Practices." *Youth and Society* 33: 62–98.

Hanushek, E. A., J. F. Kain, and S. G. Rivkin. 2004. "Why Public Schools Lose Teachers." *Journal of Human Resources* 39 (2): 326–354.

Hardy, K., and T. A. Laszloffy. 2008. "The Dynamics of a Pro-Racist Ideology: Implications for Family Therapists." In *Re-Visioning Family Therapy: Race, Culture, and Gender in Clinical Practice,* edited by M. McGoldrick and K. Hardy, 225–237. New York, NY: Guilford Press.

Harrell, S. P. 2000. "A Multidimensional Conceptualization of Racism-Related Stress: Implications for the Well-Being of People of Color." *American Journal of Orthopsychiatry* 70 (1): 42–57.

Helm, E. G., W. E. Sedlacek, and D. O. Prieto. 1998. "The Relationship between Attitudes toward Diversity and Overall Satisfaction of University Students by Race." *Journal of College Counseling* 1 (2): 111–120.

Hughes, D. 2003. "Correlates of African American and Latino Parents' Messages to Children about Ethnicity and Race: A Comparative Study of Racial Socialization." *American Journal of Community Psychology* 31 (1/2): 15–33.

Hughes, D., and L. Chen. 1997. "When and What Parents Tell Children about Race: An Examination of Race-Related Socialization among African American Families." *Applied Developmental Science* 1 (4): 200–214.

Hughes, D., and L. Chen. 1999. "The Nature of Parents' Race-Related Communications to Children: A Developmental Perspective." In *Child Psychology: A Handbook of Contemporary Issues,* edited by L. Balter and C. S. Tamis-Lemonda, 467–490. Philadelphia, PA: Psychology Press.

Jackson, C. K. 2009. "Student Demographics, Teacher Sorting and Teacher Quality: Evidence from the End of School Desegregation." *Journal of Labor Economics* 27 (2): 213–275.

Jackson, R. L., II. 1999. "Mommy, There's a Nigger at the Door." *Journal of Counseling & Development* 77: 4–6.

Laszloffy, T., and K. V. Hardy. 2000. "Uncommon Strategies for a Common Problem: Addressing Racism in Family Therapy." *Family Process* 39 (1): 35–50.

Maiter, S. 2009. "Using an Anti-Racist Framework for Assessment and Intervention in Clinical Practice with Families from Diverse Ethno-Racial Backgrounds." *Journal of Clinical Social Work* 37: 267–276.

McDowell, T. 2004. "Exploring the Racial Experience of Therapists in Training: A Critical Race Theory Perspective." *The American Journal of Family Therapy* 32: 305–324.

McDowell, T., S.-R. Fang, K. Brownlee, C. G. Young, and A. Khanna. 2002. "Transforming an MFT Program: A Model for Enhancing Diversity." *Journal of Marital and Family Therapy* 28 (2): 179–191.

McDowell, T., and D. Shelton. 2002. "Valuing Ideas of Social Justice in MFT Curricula." *Contemporary Family Therapy* 24 (2): 313–331.

McGeorge, C. R., T. S. Carlson, M. J. Erickson, and H. E. Guttormson. 2006. "Creating and Evaluating a Feminist-Informed Social Justice Couple and Family Therapy Training Model." *Journal of Feminist Family Therapy* 18 (3): 1–38.

McGoldrick, M., R. Almeida, N. G. Preto, A. Bibb, C. Sutton, J. Hudak, and P. M. Hines. 1999. "Efforts to Incorporate Social Justice Perspectives into a Family Training Program." *Journal of Marital and Family Therapy* 25 (2): 191–209.

Milem, J. F., M. J. Chang, and A. L. Antonio. 2005. *Making Diversity Work on Campus: A Research-Based Perspective.* Washington, DC: American Association of Colleges and Universities.

Mont-Reynaud, R., P. P. Ritter, and Z.-Y. Chen. 1990, March. "Correlates of Perceived Discrimination among Minority and Majority Youth in the Dornbusch-Steinberg Data Set." Paper presented at the meeting of the Society for Research on Adolescence, Atlanta, GA.

Murphy, M. J., J. Park, and N. J. Lonsdale. 2006. "Marriage and Family Therapy Students' Change in Multicultural Counseling Competencies after a Diversity Course." *Contemporary Family Therapy* 28: 303–311.

Neville, H. A., R. L. Lilly, G. Duran, R. M. Lee, and L. Browne. 2000. "Construction and Initial Validation of the Color-Blind Racial Attitudes Scale (CoBRAS)." *Journal of Counseling Psychology* 47 (1): 59–70.

Neville, H. A., R. L. Lilly, G. Duran, R. M. Lee, and L. Browne. 2001. "Race, Power, and Multicultural Counseling Psychology: Understanding White Privilege and Color-Blind Racial Attitudes." In *Handbook of Multicultural Counseling*, edited by J. G. Ponterotto, J. M. Casas, L. A. Suzuki, and C. M. Alexander, 2nd ed., 257–288. Thousand Oaks, CA: Sage.

Nosek, B. A., M. R. Banaji, and A. G. Greenwald. 2002. "Harvesting Implicit Group Attitudes and Beliefs from a Demonstration Web Site." *Group Dynamics: Theory, Research, and Practice* 6 (1): 101–115.

Obama, B. H. 2006. *The Audacity of Hope: Thoughts on Reclaiming the American Dream.* New York, NY: Random House.

Pager, D., and B. Western. 2004, December. "Race at Work: Realities of Race and Criminal Record in the NYC Job Market." Paper presented at the New York City Commission on Human Rights Conference, Schomburg Center for Research in Black Culture, New York, NY.

Phelan, J., B. G. Link, A. Stueve, and R. E. Moore. 1995. "Education, Social Liberalism, and Economic Conservatism: Attitudes toward Homeless People." *American Sociological Review* 60 (1): 126–140.

Phinney, J. S., and V. Chavira. 1995. "Parental Ethnic Socialization and Adolescent Coping with Problems Related to Ethnicity." *Journal of Research on Adolescence* 5 (1): 31–53.

Plant, E. A., and P. G. Devine. 1998. "Internal and External Motivation to Respond without Prejudice." *Journal of Personality and Social Psychology* 75: 811–832.

Schiele, J. H. 2007. "Minority Fellowship Program: Implications of the Equality-of-Oppressions Paradigm for Curriculum Content on People of Color." *Journal of Social Work* 43 (1): 83–100.

Stevenson, H. C., R. Cameron, T. Herrero-Taylor, and G. Y. Davis. 2002. "Development of the Teenager Experience of Racial Socialization Scale: Correlates of Race-Related Socialization Frequency from the Perspective of Black Youth." *Journal of Black Psychology* 28: 84–106.

Stevenson, H. C., R. Cameron, T. Herrero-Taylor, and G. Y. Davis. 2005. "Influence of Perceived Neighborhood Diversity and Racism Experience on the Racial Socialization of Black Youth." *Journal of Black Psychology* 31: 273–290.

Sue, D. W., C. M. Capodilupo, G. C. Torino, J. M. Bucceri, A. M. B. Holder, K. L. Nadal, and M. Esquilin. 2007. "Racial Microaggressions in Everyday Life: Implications for Clinical Practice." *American Psychologist* 62 (4): 271–286.

Vera, E. M., and S. L. Speight. 2003. "Multicultural Competence, Justice, and Counseling Psychology: Expanding Our Roles." *The Counseling Psychologist* 31 (3): 253–272.

Washington Post, Kaiser Family Foundation, Harvard University. 2011. *Survey of Political Independents.* Accessed March 10, 2012. http://www.washingtonpost.com/wp-srv/politics/interactives/independents/post-kaiser-harvard-topline.pdf.

Williams, D. R., and R. Williams-Morris. 2000. "Racism and Mental Health: The African-American Experience." *Ethnicity and Health* 5 (3/4): 243–268.

Wise, T. 2008. *White Like Me: Reflections on Race From a Privileged Son*, 2nd ed. Berkeley, CA: Soft Skull Press.

Wise, T. 2010. *Colorblind: The Rise of Post-Racial Politics and the Retreat from Racial Equality.* San Francisco, CA: City Lights.

Worthington, R. L., R. L. Navarro, M. Loewy, and J. Hart. 2008. "Color-Blind Racial Attitudes, Social Dominance Orientation, Racial–Ethnic Group Membership and College Students' Perceptions of Campus Climate." *Journal of Diversity in Higher Education* 1 (1): 8–19.

Zimmerman, T. S., and S. A. Haddock. 2001. "The Weave of Gender and Culture in the Tapestry of a Family Therapy Training Program: Promoting Social Justice in the Practice of Family Therapy." *Journal of Feminist Family Therapy* 12 (2): 1–31.

KIMBERLY DIGGLES received her PhD from the University of Minnesota, Twin Cities and currently works at Stanford Youth Solutions in Sacramento, CA.

The author addresses the importance of relationships in order for learning to take place in an inclusive manner. Anecdotes illustrate the value in beginning where the learner is and the unexpected opportunities the journey can lead to when both teacher and learner venture through unchartered paths together.

The Value of Connectedness in Inclusive Teaching

Ivan Figueroa

In today's society, we tend to think of learning taking place in a formal or institutional setting such as schools and universities. However, learning takes place continuously, everywhere, and at all ages (Jeffs and Smith 1997). Unfortunately, most people tend to associate formal or institutional learning with a prescribed or regimented learning. A learning that dictates what is to be learned, when it is to be learned, and at what pace it should proceed. A learning that does not allow the freedom to explore, a learning that is not innate, that does not follow the curiosity that we all have from the time we are born. "A sad part of most education is that by the time our children have spent a number of years in school, this intrinsic motivation is pretty well dampened" (Rogers 1994, 186). Not all of us respond to the structures and demarcations imposed on us in institutionalized learning the same way, and, as a result, this system has dichotomized us into categories of learners, such as "exceptional learners" or "at-risk learners." As a result, many of us have bought into these categories attributed to us, and those labeled as "at risk" or "vulnerable" become marginalized. This group then comes to believe they cannot learn or are not good at learning, and dreams of a college degree disappear. Thus, there are a large "number of people [in the world] who are excluded from meaningful participation in the economic, social, political, and cultural life of their communities" (UNESCO 2003, 3).

There are many learning styles, preferences, learning strategies, and conditions under which our learning flourishes. Not everyone learns the same way and sometimes we look for ways to approach things that are new to us. Given the proper conditions, our learning has a greater potential to proceed unfettered. "Inclusive education as an approach seeks to address

NEW DIRECTIONS FOR TEACHING AND LEARNING, no. 140, Winter 2014 © 2014 Wiley Periodicals, Inc.
Published online in Wiley Online Library (wileyonlinelibrary.com) • DOI: 10.1002/tl.20112

45

the learning needs of all children, youth and adults with a specific focus on those who are vulnerable to marginalization and exclusion" (UNESCO 2003, 4). Booth describes inclusive education as "the process of increasing the participation of students in the cultures and curricula of mainstream schools and communities; it is the process of reducing the exclusion of students from mainstream cultures and curricula" (Booth 1996, 89). Inclusive learning is "concerned with providing appropriate responses to the broad spectrum of learning needs in formal and non-formal educational settings" (UNESCO 2003, 7). "It aims to enable both teachers and learners to feel comfortable with diversity and to see it as a challenge and enrichment in the learning environment, rather than a problem" (UNESCO 2003, 7). Inclusive teaching and learning seek to create and encourage an atmosphere of freedom to learn, where the prior knowledge and experiences of the learner are the foundations upon which new knowledge and new experiences are built. This kind of teaching and learning environment helps students to better understand how they learn best and empowers them with the abilities to make personal connections, connecting current knowledge to the information being taught.

Still, for inclusive learning to take place, it must be intentional. The facilitator must make an effort to strike a connection so that existing barriers to learning can help to be breached, and the learner learns how to take control of his or her own learning, overcome personal barriers to learning, learn from everyday experiences, and know the conditions under which they learn best (Smith 1982). This connection does not occur in any prescribed manner, nor can the time it will take be predicted. Each individual learns at his or her own pace. The challenge to learn is greater for those who no longer believe nor trust their capability to learn. However, breaking down the belief that one is not capable of learning *can* be overcome with time and effort.

My experience has been that this is a process. It does not occur instantaneously through the acknowledgement that we are all unique in our learning process. The application of the assumptions of andragogy, "the art and science of helping adults learn" (Knowles 1970, 38), is of great importance for success. Malcolm Knowles proposed six assumptions of the characteristics of adult learners "to be checked out in terms of their rightness for particular learners in particular situations" (Knowles, Holton, and Swanson 1998, 96). These assumptions are that: (1) adults have a need to know why they need to learn something before undertaking to learn it; (2) adults are increasingly self-directing; (3) the learner's experience is a rich resource for learning; (4) the adult's readiness to learn develops from life tasks and problems; (5) an adult's orientation to learning is task or problem centered; and (6) an adult's motivation to learn is driven by internal factors (Knowles 1993). In order for *meaningful* learning to take place, both the facilitator and the learner must deal with most of these assumptions either consciously or unconsciously.

I met a young man when I was an adjunct, teaching foreign language courses. This young man had worked in the oil fields and been a musician in a band. Like many students I have met throughout my career, he knew if he wanted to improve his opportunities he needed to further his education, and ultimately he made the decision to take a few college courses. We began striking up conversations, and, as I got to know him better, I learned that he was the first in his family to attend college, and, in addition to his working part time at the college, he was also doing custodial and maintenance work in the evenings. Our conversations touched on a lot of different topics, from his classroom experiences with students to his interactions with faculty. As time passed, I discovered he had a keen interest in literature and poetry. I encouraged him to pursue an associate's degree, as this would give him that added credential he was seeking. He gradually began to ask more and more questions about college and higher education. He had an inquisitive mind and wanted to gain a better understanding of how it worked. Eventually, he made the decision to transfer to a land grant university where he pursued a degree in English literature.

Academic performance never became an issue; his curiosity and love for literature kept him moving forward. Our conversations continued throughout his journey, most centered on the challenges of navigating faculty who would speak down to him and classmates who came from privileged homes who taxed his patience with their topics of conversation about where to spend spring break. Coming from a working class background there was always a sense of not fitting in, and he was always confronting challenging bouts with feelings of inadequacy. Years went by, but he finally obtained his degree. I saw his extraordinary writing skills and his perceptivity, so I encouraged him to consider graduate school; however, doubts continued to plague him. He took a full-time position at a college in student support services, and had it not been for the pressure of paying back student loans with a meager salary, probably he would not have given it serious consideration. He did enroll in graduate school and soon realized that when you find your passion, no matter how challenging the work, one does find it easy to do. The coursework came easy to him, and the learning was enjoyed. The feelings of inadequacy still haunted him from time to time, but a growing and stronger sense of being capable of doing the work and producing scholarship took the lead. The degree was completed successfully, and he is now weighing new choices: to pursue his PhD or work and pay off some of the enormous student loan debt.

The following occurred with a student in another class. One year I was teaching a night course at a community college. Many of the students who enrolled in this course were nontraditional students and working adults, much like the man I will now describe. This man had spent a number of years working his way through college. I noticed that at times he would be deeply engaged in the class and at other times distracted and tired. I thought nothing of it because this was not unusual for the working adult. Through conversations we had during breaks, I came to learn that he had attention deficit hyperactivity disorder (ADHD), and this was his third college. He was determined to complete his degree and would bring a laptop to class. He expressed how difficult it was for him to take notes and follow explanations indicating that if he concentrated on the explanation, then he could not take notes that were useful to him, and if he focused on taking notes, he had difficulty following the flow of the explanations. Over time he told me about his experiences in school. From an early age, teachers would single him out because he would fidget, not even realizing it; his behavior was considered disruptive, and he was always getting into trouble with his teachers. After a number of consultations, the school officials recommended to his parents that he be put on Ritalin. This did help control his hyperactivity, but he expressed how he hated the effect it had on him, summing it up with "I couldn't feel." His grades were average, and he got in a lot less trouble with his teachers. As soon as he completed high school he stopped taking the Ritalin. College was different for him; most of the time he worked either part time or full time. As he put it, things would come up, so there were semesters where he got through, and other times he would have to withdraw from class because he was not doing well. When I met him he had just gotten off academic probation. He did not return to my class after midterm and withdrew from the course feeling he could not complete it successfully. However, he continued to see me at my office and tell me how he was doing academically and personally. Throughout our continued conversations, I came to learn that he had many challenges to learning; besides his diagnosed ADHD he also struggled with obsessive-compulsive behavior, depression, and, as a result, bouts with alcohol abuse. Although he was convinced of his intellectual ability, his experiences throughout school with teachers caused doubts, leading him to believe that he was marginal when it came to his academic abilities in college at best. We began to explore resources and strategies to assist in his academic endeavors. Visits with the Office for Learning Disabilities provided note-taking strategies and technological resources. He also took advantage of campus counseling services that led to a referral to a psychiatrist, who with detailed attention prescribed medication that did not have the same side effects as the Ritalin. Working with counseling services created a pathway that allowed him to work through many of the root causes of his depression and develop coping strategies. Gradually, he began to acquire more of a balance in his personal life, and his grades improved. We traveled this road together; I gained insights into challenges to learning that I previously only had intellectual knowledge about, and, through encouragement and support that I would provide, he dealt head on with matters that he had avoided throughout his life. This young man has graduated with a college degree, has a successful career, and is now beginning a new phase in his life learning to be a loving and supportive husband and father.

These anecdotes do not eloquently convey that inclusive teaching and learning entail a vested commitment to join the learner's journey. The accounts oversimplify the time and efforts to demonstrate and receive the investment into individual lives: the development of trust, the partnership to the learning, and the mentor–mentee relationship that evolves and eventually ends as the mentee grows and achieves.

Being aware and sensitive to all learners and adjusting our teaching to factor in each student's prior experiences and needs as a starting point in the journey of the learning transaction are essential for inclusive teaching and learning. As someone whose job is to impart knowledge, it is up to us to be inclusive in the way we teach and to find a way to connect with our students. The end results are not always what the mentor expects as the best path for the mentee to take. However, what is the heart of the matter is what works best for the learner. Key to these relationships is the belief in the capacity of the learner to learn. Students CAN learn, but it is up to us to find a way to reach them, because if we do not believe in them, what chance do they have of reaching their full potential?

References

Booth, T. 1996. "A Perspective on Inclusion from England." *Cambridge Journal of Education* 26 (1): 87–99.

Jeffs, T., and M. K. Smith. 1997. "What is Informal Education?" *The Encyclopedia of Informal Education*. http://infed.org/mobi/what-is-informal-education/.

Knowles, M. S. 1970. *The Modern Practice of Adult Education: Andragogy Versus Pedagogy*. New York, NY: Association Press.

Knowles, M. S. 1993. "Contributions of Malcolm Knowles." In *The Christian Educator's Handbook on Adult Education*, edited by K. O. Gangel and J. C. Wilhoit, 91–103. Grand Rapids, MI: Baker Books.

Knowles, M. S., E. F. Holton, and R. A. Swanson. 1998. *The Adult Learner*. Houston, TX: Gulf Publishing Company.

Rogers, C. R. 1994. *Freedom to Learn*. Upper Saddle River, NJ: Prentice-Hall.

Smith, R. M. 1982. *Learning How to Learn*. Chicago, IL: Follett Publishing Company.

UNESCO. 2003. *Overcoming Exclusion through Inclusive Approaches in Education*. Accessed December 17, 2013. http://unesdoc.unesco.org/images/0013/001347/134785e.pdf.

IVAN FIGUEROA *is the director of the Mountaineer Scholars Program and Diversity Initiatives at Southern Vermont College in Bennington, Vermont.*

NEW DIRECTIONS FOR TEACHING AND LEARNING • DOI: 10.1002/tl

6

In a context that is increasingly becoming more diverse, we consider it essential to promote activities to develop linguistic and cultural awareness among preservice teachers. This chapter is based on the narratives of college students who when enrolled in an English as a Second Language class participated in a project where they accompanied newly resettled refugee families on their first visit to their children's school. Using narrative inquiry, the authors analyze the students' experience and describe the impact it had on them. The students' reflections provide evidence of their developing cultural awareness. The authors conclude that teacher educators can engage preservice students in authentic experience aimed at developing cultural awareness.

A Journey with a Refugee Family: Raising Culturally Relevant Teaching Awareness

Freyca Calderon Berumen, Cecilia Silva

Introduction

I never had an experience like that ever. It was the first time I really inter-acted one-on-one with a family. It's not just a family, but a family that doesn't speak English very well, from another country, completely different culture and so, that was a huge kind of learning experience for me, but I enjoyed this experience so much. It was ... it warmed my heart, being able to see the things that I could do, like just taking a family to their children's school to see what they're actually getting there and seeing their faces light up and learning about all the different cultural aspects that affect education as well.

Meaningful, authentic, and *eye opening* are some of the words preservice teachers used to describe a structured experience they had in one of our classes. In this chapter, we discuss a project that preservice teachers completed when enrolled in an English as a Second Language (ESL) course that we teach. The project aims at developing a better understanding of refugee children and their families as they settle in our community. It is our intent to highlight the significance the project had on the college students' preparation and the difference it made in their developing awareness of culturally relevant teaching practices.

NEW DIRECTIONS FOR TEACHING AND LEARNING, no. 140, Winter 2014 © 2014 Wiley Periodicals, Inc.
Published online in Wiley Online Library (wileyonlinelibrary.com) • DOI: 10.1002/tl.20114

Culturally Relevant Teaching

Culturally relevant teaching (CRT) hinges on the premise that people learn differently across cultures and that previous experiences are fundamental for knowledge construction (Banks 2001; Ladson-Billings 1995). To enhance learning, teachers must understand the importance of taking account of the background knowledge of all the cultures represented in their classrooms. To elucidate what CRT means, we want to clarify that culture is dynamic, complex, interactive, and changing, yet a stabilizing force in human life (Gay 2010).

Erickson (2010) affirms that everything in education relates to culture, saying "Culture is in us and all around us, just as is the air we breathe. In its scope and distribution, it is personal, familial, communal, institutional, societal, and global" (35). Individuals shape their identity through their home culture and the culture that surrounds them. As educators, we cannot be unresponsive to cultures within a classroom that consequently impact learning outcomes.

For Gay (2010), CRT involves "using the cultural knowledge, prior experiences, frames of reference, and performance styles of ethnically diverse students to make learning encounters more relevant to and effective for them" (31). She described six central characteristics that CRT comprises: validating and affirming, comprehensive, multidimensional, empowering, transformative, and emancipatory. CRT is validating and affirming because it acknowledges the legitimacy of all cultures and takes into account home and community experiences as meaningful for learning construction. CRT is comprehensive because it works on all the aspects of child development. CRT is multidimensional as it encompasses the various dimensions of students' learning, such as curriculum content, classroom and school environment, several forms of assessments, and even extracurricular activities. CRT is empowering as students gain self-confidence and develop skills and competencies to achieve academic success. It is transformative as it demands creativity to go beyond conventional forms of teaching to include the life experiences of diverse students as part of their learning. CRT is emancipatory for it liberates students from mainstream stereotypes.

CRT aims to unfold all the learning potentials of diverse students to the fullest by validating and affirming their cultural identity. In a context like Texas, a state increasingly becoming more diverse, teacher educators must help preservice teachers develop awareness about linguistic and cultural differences. This process requires that they interact with the families of the students they will be teaching in schools. Such interaction is particularly important for middle/secondary education majors because they seldom have opportunities to meet their students' parents, especially if they come from linguistic and cultural backgrounds different from their own.

NEW DIRECTIONS FOR TEACHING AND LEARNING • DOI: 10.1002/tl

Refugees in Texas

Welcoming more refugees than any other state in 2011, Texas resettled 5,623 refugees—approximately 10 percent of the total number of those arriving to the United States (Freemantle 2012). Arriving from all over the world, the majority of refugees currently resettling in Texas originate from Burma, Bhutan, and Iraq. In Texas, the Refugee Resettlement Program provides housing, medical assistance, and social services—employment, education, vocational training, and ESL—to refugees for a determined period of time (Texas Health and Human Services Commission n.d.). A number of local community agencies that assist refugees in integrating into American culture manage these programs.

A refugee is someone who has been forced to flee his or her country of origin because of persecution, war, or violence based on race, religion, nationality, or political interests. For these reasons, refugees cannot return to their home country and must seek protection elsewhere. Although refugees wait for a country to accept their application to obtain refugee status, they settle temporarily in another country, often one neighboring their country of origin. The waiting period is indeterminate. Some refugees may wait for just a few weeks, whereas others may wait for years. The United Nations High Commissioner for Refugees (UNHCR) organizes all efforts to coordinate refugee resettlement at the international level.

The living conditions of refugees differ depending on their temporary placement while waiting for resettlement to a new country. Many of these initial placements do not have enough resources to meet basic living needs, let alone provide a good education for the children. When working with refugee children, one needs to understand that many of them have experienced harsh living conditions from war and violence in their countries and extreme levels of poverty in their refugee camps. Consequently, refugee children resettling in the United States may have had limited or no access to formal schooling. Schools in the United States generally place refugee children in a particular grade level according to their age, often ignoring the fact that their grade-level placement might be above their level of education. To help us focus on the educational needs of many of the refugee children, Gahungu, Gahungu, and Luseno (2011) propose that we adopt the term "culturally displaced students with truncated formal education" (3). Placing recently arrived refugees in a mainstream classroom is very likely to set them up for failure unless school administrators and teachers practice a culturally responsive pedagogy. In this sense, it is very important that pre- and in-service teachers understand the particular circumstances of refugee students.

In our locality, one of the community agencies working with refugees joined efforts with the local school district to meet the educational needs of these children. Consequently, refugee children attend a newcomer school designed to help newly arrived students—immigrants and refugees—

NEW DIRECTIONS FOR TEACHING AND LEARNING • DOI: 10.1002/tl

develop English and the academic skills necessary for transitioning into their neighborhood schools. Given the educational needs of the public school children in our locality, our university teacher preparation program collaborates with the newcomer school and the community agency in developing cultural and linguistic awareness for preservice teachers enrolled in our teacher preparation program.

Refugee Family Project

Working in collaboration with the newcomer school and one of the resettlement agencies in our community, we centered this project around a family visit to the newcomer school. We matched preservice students with a recently arrived family who had children enrolled at the newcomer school. Grouped in pairs, the college students coordinated the school visit and accompanied the family using public transportation to an orientation session at the newcomer school and back to their home. The project had four components:

1. Students conducted research on the country of origin of the refugee family. For this part of the assignment they considered information that would benefit a teacher working with a particular refugee family group (that is, historical context/reasons for resettlement, ethnicity, culture/traditional practices, religion, language, education, social background, and so on).
2. The students and families met for the first time at a family dinner. Organized in committees, the students identified and planned the various tasks needed to carry out the family dinner (for example, budget, food selection and purchase, setup and cleanup, introduction to the project, translators, and so on). In addition to allowing students and families to interact and build trust, the dinner provided a chance for the students and families to agree on a date and time for the school visit.
3. Students met the family at their home and accompanied its members to the school. With the assistance of personnel from the newcomer school, the students and the families conducted a school tour and became familiar with general school routines.
4. Students wrote a reflection that describes their learning experience.

Methodology

We framed this study using qualitative inquiry, which allows researchers, participants, and readers to seek an understanding of a particular event, situation, or phenomenon. Qualitative inquiry relies on interpretation and experiences, and it varies from one context to another. Narrative inquiry is a way of understanding experience (Given 2008). Hence, this study uses narratives of personal interpretations as participants thoroughly described their personal experience and made meaning of their participation in the project.

The samples for this study are the preservice teachers who had enrolled in an ESL class during the fall semesters of 2011 and 2012. We conducted interviews with a total of ten students. Participants were all female; six were seniors completing certification requirements for middle and secondary English education, and four were graduate students completing an accelerated master's program (four-year undergraduate/one-year graduate) in special education at the time of the experience. We examined the transcripts of the interviews through a thematic analysis to identify patterns, code data units, and create categories that helped us understand the experiences (Guest, MacQueen, and Namey 2011).

Findings

Six themes emerged from the thematic analysis of the student interviews. Through these themes, we see that the preservice students, through their self-reflections, are beginning to develop a personal and professional consciousness about the linguistic and cultural diversity of families with whom they engage during the project.

We Were Prepared with All Sorts of Things, but ...   To provide college students with a context for the process of integrating refugee families into the community, staff from the resettlement agency conducted an introductory presentation prior to the family dinner. The presentation highlighted background as to the work of the office of the UNHCR in coordinating international efforts to protect and assist refugee families. The staff discussed the kind of work that agencies like theirs do to help families in becoming self-sufficient and offered a number of resources to support the students' research for the project (see the Appendix).

When preparing for the family dinner, students had to consider the kind of food that would be appropriate to serve because the families would most likely have dietary restrictions and might not consume pork or beef. In addition to menus, students worked on the general logistics involved in planning and serving the dinner (for example, setup, serving, cleanup, and so on). Because we knew that the families participating in the project were Nepali and Burmese (Karen and Karenni), one of the committees made arrangements to have two translators from the community agency present at the dinner to facilitate communication. At this point in the preparation, students also considered ways to best introduce the project to the families and gifts they could offer in appreciation for their willingness to be part of the experience.

The students organized themselves into planning committees based on the resources and experiences each could bring to the planning task. The committees not only gave the students a sense of accountability for the success of the project, but it also moved the experience beyond the "typical"

ESL course assignment. One of the students reflected on the value of the committees in terms of their authenticity:

> I feel like *authentic* is the best word to describe it. It felt authentic because it didn't feel like a school project. [...] We were actually doing something in the community and we got to work together and we were dealing with real money, real budgets and communicating to outside caterers and companies, so it was really cool and really rewarding to see, to get to experience it and meet all the families there.

Every week, we devoted the first part of the class to updates on the various committees. In spite of this planning, students were still feeling uneasy about the family dinner. One of the students recalled, "We were prepared with all sorts of things, but I still had no idea what to expect." A second student remarked on how this feeling lingered until the night of the family dinner: "It was like even up until that point it was very abstract, oh these families, but I couldn't even picture what they would look like or know like what it would be like."

I Was Nervous because of the Language Barrier.   Anticipating ways to bridge the language barrier, students prepared a variety of visual aids to support communication during the dinner. In spite of being prepared, the students expressed that they were feeling anxious about their ability to initially communicate with the families at the dinner: "At first I was really scared. I was nervous because the language barrier, kind of, freaks me out."

One of the committees decided that it would be a good idea to cover the tables with butcher paper and have crayons available, a practice they had often seen in restaurants. Several of the students used the crayons to draw pictures and play games such as tic-tac-toe with the children. These activities turned out to be a good icebreaker for everyone in the family groups. These simple materials were invaluable in bolstering communication as the various groups used them to support their attempts to communicate throughout the evening.

Once everyone finished dinner, the committee in charge of introducing the project began a formal presentation. For this part of the program, the students had prepared PowerPoint slides. As they discussed each slide, the two translators interpreted what the students were communicating to the families. The committee in charge of the presentation was very much aware of the need to simplify the language and use many images to illustrate the journey to and from the newcomer school. Following the formal presentation, each group was to identify a time and date to visit the newcomer school. One of the students described how she prepared for the event:

> I had made some visuals before we went to dinner. I printed out a map and circled their apartments and the school, and drew a line with a little bus on it, so that they knew where we were going. And then I printed out a calendar and circled the day, and put the time. And so I let her [the mother] keep those.

Reflecting on their own nervousness about meeting and interacting with the families, the students noted that the parents probably had similar feelings coming into the dinner: "I think the parents were just as nervous as we were, and they felt just as awkward so, I mean, it just was something that you, kind of, just had to dive into and hope for the best." This sense of empathy for the family is also evident in the following statement:

> Communication is how I interact with, learn more about, and build relation-
> ships with new people; how was I going to do any of this with the family I
> was paired up with? When the day finally came and I arrived at the family's
> apartment complex, I had some clarity. The nervousness and anxiousness I
> had felt about being put in this situation was nothing compared to the ner-
> vousness and anxiousness this family had felt as refugees being placed in a
> completely foreign country to begin an entirely new life.

Throughout the experience, students found that hand and facial gestures, as well as body expression, often served as the best communication aids: "And so body language was just a huge deal at the dinner. We smiled a lot, and probably felt awkward doing … smiling so much and using a bunch of hand gestures, but we just had to, in order to communicate."

As one might expect, the communication challenges went beyond the family dinner. The bus ride to the school proved to be the context where hand gestures and facial expressions became excellent resources in bridging communication: "And they, you know, obviously spoke Nepali and so at this point we couldn't communicate with them per se as far as language, but we had a lot of communication … facial, you know, expressions and hand gestures." Smiles again abounded throughout the bus ride: "It was a lot of smiling and nodding." However, the students were not the only ones who found smiles useful; so did the families: "[They would] look at us and smile even though they couldn't talk in English."

The students brought up the role of silence in communication in many of the interviews. Being silent, the students observed, made them feel uncomfortable: "but I think at the beginning we just didn't want there to be any silence. It was super awkward and by the end of the day we felt a little more like okay." For another student, the awkwardness of silence transformed into an opportunity for reflection: "I think that was kind of actually healthy for us to have those silent moments to ourselves to kind of collect and think about what was happening and take it all in."

In attempting to break the awkwardness of silence, another student discovered that her mobile technology was a good conduit through which she may establish a common tie with one of the mothers:

> How were we going to have conversation? We don't speak the same language.
> And so, I thought it was weird that we weren't saying anything to each other
> and so I got out my phone and I had some pictures on my phone and so, I

showed her a picture of my baby cousin, which I think she actually thought was my baby, but I tried to explain, no, not mine. And her face, … she was … like she could relate because she knew that, you know, she had kids and I showed her a couple of other pictures.

As part of the bus riding experience, focusing on the use of a variety of communicative strategies helped students reflect on the level of energy—physical as well as cognitive and emotional—that it takes to bridge communication gaps. On this point, a student said:

I think maybe just recognizing that communication, kind of takes everything, like you have to mentally be processing things and thinking things out emotionally and socially, like try to make it a comfortable environment but then also physically interact with them.

In the end, it became apparent to the students that they were capable of applying many of the communicative strategies they often used in the classroom with beginning English language learners (ELLs): "It was really just us using our resources and what we were learning to be able to interact with them and help them in some way and it was really neat how we did it too."

I've Never Been on the Bus. One of the salient outcomes of the project was the impact that the experience of riding the bus with the family had on the students. As part of the services provided to refugees, the resettlement agency and the local transportation authority collaborate to support newly arrived families in learning how to use mass transit. This support involves getting to know local routes as well as the general mechanics of using public transit (for example, boarding the bus, paying fares, making transfers, and so on). An employee of the transit authority is available to accompany the families on their first journey using the bus services.

In preparation for the bus ride, we asked the college students to contact the public transit agent to make arrangements to meet at the families' apartment complex on the date and time they had prearranged for the school visit. In spite of the fact that the students were aware that the agent was going to accompany the group on the bus trip, in addition to being anxious about their ability to communicate with the family, their unfamiliarity with the bus system added to their uneasiness:

I'd never been on the bus, I've never been to their apartment complex, and I've never been on that side of town. So I think it was just the unknown that made me nervous, and the language.

The students' lack of experience with the bus system put them on the same playing field as the families:

[The mom] was nervous because she felt like we knew everything and we were like leading her, but we really didn't know what we were doing either. We wanted to communicate that to her because we wanted her to be like we're on the same level, we're in this together, but that's a pretty difficult emotion to express.

Unlike citizens of other urban cities, most people in our community make use of private cars for transportation. On average, a one-way bus ride from the family's apartment complex to the school takes one and a half hours and it involves one bus transfer. That is, assuming the buses are running on time, a round trip between home and school involves a minimum of three hours. The same route, the students were quick to note, would take them 20–25 minutes—one way—if they used their own car. This realization prompted many of the students to reflect on the trials that transportation poses for families as they conduct everyday chores:

As we were riding we had so much time to think, we're thinking about all the things that would change if you didn't have your own transportation because you'd have to move your schedule around and then we're thinking like for grocery shopping even, you'd have to take all your groceries on the bus and if you have kids, I don't know, it just seems pretty crazy.

One of the students considered the effects that transportation could have on families from the perspective of a teacher when requesting classroom supplies:

But I think it helped to realize what lengths people go to, to do simple tasks because just thinking about sending home school supplies, saying that your kid needs to bring the poster board to school this week, figuring out the bus system to take you to somewhere that's close to a supply store, and then to have the funding to buy the poster, and then bring all your materials home, working around a bus schedule, a work schedule.

The bus ride provided the students an opportunity to reflect on their understanding of their own community. It presented a place and culture with which they were familiar in unfamiliar ways, making it as foreign to them as it was to the families:

It felt kind of like a different world. Even when we pulled into the main station in downtown where all the other ones branch out, I actually said to [partner's name], I feel like we're in a different country. I've been to some train stations in Europe and I was like it felt kind of like that.

The bus ride also allowed students to consider issues of equity. Often when students reflected on their own privilege they used the expression *living in a bubble*:

> It was just eye opening to the fact that I'm here in my bubble at [university's name], and that those kids don't have the same experience that I do. It just really opened me up as far as worldly knowledge, and I've travelled extensively and I felt like, oh, I know, I've been on a bus, you know, I figured it out, but it was very foreign to be and see places I know; when I'm riding on the bus, I have a completely different experience going through, as I'm looking through the windows.

Do I Have to Take My Shoes Off before I Go into the Apartment? In preparation for the dinner, the students had researched general cultural traditions of the families. Wanting to be culturally appropriate, the background research became more meaningful in anticipation of the school visit. One student said, "I learned that my family was from Burma and after meeting them, I feel like I Googled everything on the planet, because I didn't want to be in any way rude or cross any boundaries or offend anybody."

Not wanting to disrespect the families created a sense of insecurity for many of the students:

> It was really difficult and I was confused if I was doing the right thing, saying the right words in the right way, you know, but overall in the end it was a huge heart-warming experience and all that kind of stress of finding where to go, what to do, what to say, you know … do I walk into the apartment? Do I have to take my shoes off before I go into the apartment?

The stress of dealing with a new culture, as noted by the student in the previous quote, is commonly known as cultural fatigue—the feeling of exhaustion that results from constantly attempting to adjust to cultural differences. Without having to travel far from their own community, these students repeatedly acknowledged feeling culturally fatigued:

> It's mentally stressful I think, to just always be analyzing, okay did I do something offensive? Is there anything I've just done that could in some way be construed as offensive […]?

In the family groups where males participated in the school visit, students noticed different dynamics in terms of the ways in which the males positioned themselves in the bus. They attributed this behavior to cross-cultural gender differences. One student noted how "they [the males] sat towards the back of the bus and [student's name] and I sat with two of the mothers towards the front of the bus." The mothers in this group would even "pat the seat in front of them like sit next to us and they wanted us to be near them and interacting with them like that." On the return trip, while the seating arrangements in the bus changed slightly, there was still a distance between the males and the females: "whenever we got back on the bus, the mothers sat down, I noticed that the men sat a little closer to us, but they still didn't sit with us."

For a second group, the seating arrangement proved to be more dramatic. This was apparent in their description of the way the father they were accompanying to school chose to sit away from the two college students when boarding the bus:

> And so we got on the bus and we sat down on a row where there were plenty of seats for all of us to sit together, and he kept walking and sat, like, five rows behind us, and we were … we were really confused, like, what are we going to do?

The distancing was even more evident as the group approached the school after leaving the bus stop:

> The dad, the whole time, even from when we got off at the final bus stop, he was kind of, away … not too far but a little, he was walking behind us, probably ten to 15 feet behind us, and we tried to slow down and when we would slow down and try to get closer, he would slow down too, like, really, really purposefully keeping that distance from us.

Their Faces Lit Up.   "Parents just don't care" is a remark often made by classroom teachers ignorant of the factors that preclude linguistically and culturally diverse families from engaging in traditional parent involvement roles in schools. One can often attribute what often appears to be a lack of caring to parents having different perceptions of the ways in which they care and get involved in their children's education and to socioeconomic and educational factors affecting immigrant and refugee families (Li 2013). Recognizing that parents do care, students considered some of these factors in their reflections:

> I think understanding how parents feel and that there are other things going on at home, that's not just that they don't want to be there, that they don't value education. It's that sometimes there are things that outrank that, so just figuring out a bus system in a new place, there's a language barrier, and just cultural roles as well.

Given the language barriers, the students captured the notion of "caring" through descriptions of the family's physical reaction to situations that triggered this feeling: "You could see their faces light up." One of the students reminisced about the moment a mother and her son saw each other at the newcomer school:

> I remember just walking down the hall with the mom and all of a sudden this little kid comes up and hugs her and her face lit up so bright and she hadn't smiled really that big yet in that day.

The interviews disclosed various moments at which the college students had firsthand experiences observing the parents' sense of pride. One student described the parents' reaction to a display of their child's work on the hallway walls: "whenever they were looking at his work, they seemed genuinely interested … and they were really, really, proud of what he had accomplished in such a short time." Similarly, another student described a mother's reaction after first seeing her child at the school:

> She reached over and hugged him and put her arm around his shoulders and kind of hugged him like she was proud of him and they all had huge smiles on their faces so you could tell they were obviously very proud.

The students were able to observe how parents demonstrate caring even in the case where the father they were accompanying to the newcomer school had been reticent to interact with them. The father's expression, the students noted, radically changed as he saw his son at the school:

> The other son was in junior high, middle school, and so we went to see him in there, in like the basement part of the school, and we went down there, and as soon as we got there, that was the first time we saw the dad smile and show emotion, and his smile was the length of his face, to see his other son in the class, and so that son got to come out with us and we went to meet some of his teachers and, they were praising the student, saying they're really good workers.

In one instance, a group of students was able to receive direct feedback from a parent about the school visit. This group, unlike any of the other family groups, happened to have a parent who had been a teacher in Nepal and spoke some English. As the group was leaving the school, they asked him for feedback about the trip to the school. He responded, "They were overwhelmed, appreciative, and thankful that their children have been given the opportunity to get a good education, something they were not afforded in Nepal."

Overall, the students reflected on their heightened understanding of the need to take parent perspectives into consideration:

> As an educator, I think it opened me up to parent perspective within the classroom, and not only for students of refugee families, but just in general.

Just getting to know students' parents as far as life goes on outside of your classroom, that you can't prejudge and you can't think that they don't care, they didn't come, they didn't respond to my email, and that kind of stuff. I think it's important to realize that there might be a language barrier, that they might be working two to three jobs at home, that there might not be a mom at home.

Now I Can.   In their narratives, students identified the project as significant in terms of their growing confidence in reaching out to parents. Given their own socioeconomic and educational backgrounds, many of the preservice educators enrolled in the class never expected to work with ELLs, much less interact with their families: "Honestly, right when we first started I was like, I'm probably never going to have a student that's not going to know any English. I'm, like, okay, this probably is never going to happen to me."

When looking back at the experience, this same student contrasted her naïve initial expectations to the reality of her student teaching placement and reflected on her ability to engage with parents as a direct result from the project:

> Now, I have, … parents who don't speak English at all. And so, it's been hard but I've always had that experience in the back of my mind, … And most of them have come to the open house or some event at the school where I have been able to meet them face to face and try to talk with them and explain what's going on.

In another interview, a student remarked that even though professors throughout her teacher preparation program had always advocated for parent involvement, up until this experience she had not felt comfortable communicating with parents, particularly if non-English speaking. In the interview, she commented on her newfound sense of confidence: "It just helped knowing that after I accomplished this, that I can reach out and I can communicate, even when I felt like I couldn't."

On a similar note, a different student expressed how she is now reconsidering her ability to make home visits. Prior to the experience with the refugee family, she would have been too frightened to do so. Although this type of insight is critical for all classroom teachers, we believe it is particularly significant for middle and secondary educators because often teachers working with students at these levels do not have many opportunities to interact with parents.

Conclusion and Recommendations

Our findings suggest that the project provided preservice educators with the opportunity to develop a deeper understanding of the process of resettlement for refugee children and their families as well as new perspectives to support them in creating a culturally relevant classroom. Engaging in real-life experiences such as this one, as Gay and Kirkland (2003) point out, not only makes learning genuine and authentic, but increases the probability that preservice educators avoid the intellectual, emotional, psychological, and moral challenges involved in creating critical consciousness and self-reflection.

The project had some unanticipated outcomes. For teachers at the newcomer school, the family visit also provided an opportunity to address concerns regarding children with their parents. In one case, the teacher had been unsuccessful in his attempts to contact the family to discuss some of the academic difficulties that one of the children was having at school. At the school visit, however, he was able to talk to the mother, and as a result the student began to participate in the after-school tutoring sessions offered by the refugee resettlement agency at the school. In another case, a teacher was concerned about a child who was not eating at all during the school day. After the meeting, they started sending lunch from home, so that their son would have food that he was familiar with and liked while he became accustomed to the food choices offered at the school cafeteria.

The second unforeseen result was that students identified the project as an asset in terms of their own preparation to be classroom teachers during hiring interviews. When participating in job teaching fairs, if asked questions related to the strengths or unique experiences that would distinguish them from other applicants, they often made reference to the project. One student said:

> Just speaking about this [the class project] has helped me to open up to a view that I don't think most people get within an interview, that I can put myself in a situation I might not be comfortable in, but that it's okay and that I can reach out to people who don't speak English or might not be accustomed to [American] norms.

Reflecting on the job interviewing process, another student was excited that prospective employers asked her over and over again to talk about her experience with the family: "I don't think they've ever heard of anything like this going on, so I think they enjoyed just hearing something different, and getting this experience that most people have no experience with." The interest showed by school administrators hiring new teachers, while unanticipated by us, also suggested that the outcomes of this experience are critical in terms of the background knowledge and experiences schools seek in their new teachers. This value-added feature of the project is an incentive to keep working and building on this experience.

Drawing from our experience, we identify some important features that other teacher educators might want to consider if exploring the possibility of developing initiatives similar to the one we discuss in this chapter. First, it is essential to establish partnerships with other organizations in the community. We have a long history of collaboration with the resettlement agency and see the collaboration as benefiting both parties. Although our students profit from the agency's history and experience in working with refugees, they also work with the agency in supporting its new arrivals in connecting to schools and learning to use the transit system. Through our interviews, we also found out that two of the students who were enrolled in our class continued working with the agency as volunteers and now regularly tutor refugee children through the after-school program at the newcomer school.

Similarly, the support of the newcomer school has also been instrumental to the project. The newcomer school's outreach educators initially identified and contacted the families that participated in the school visit, and the classroom teachers were more than willing to interact with the visiting families as they toured the school campus. The preservice educators who participate in this project also concurrently complete a semester-long practicum at the school. As we consider future collaborations, we are also exploring the possibility of having the high school students from the newcomer school visit our campus, thus supporting the school's efforts in developing a college-going culture.

The second key component critical to this project is to have the disposition to deal with a certain degree of uncertainty. As we discussed before, the unknown was a constant in the narratives—the students experienced a high level of anxiety due to the unknown parts of the project. Although we cannot control a number of aspects in a project such as this one, one of the big issues is communication. In spite of all of the planning, for example, some of the preservice educators arrived at the families' apartment only to find that the family was not ready to go on the school visit and had to reschedule the trip. In other cases, the preservice educators arrived at the apartment complex expecting to accompany one family only to find that other family groups had decided to join the group. Or, as it happened with one particular group, the family had found its own transportation to the school and had already left the complex by the time the preservice students arrived to their apartment. Problems with communication, however, were not limited to our inability to anticipate how much English the families knew. In order for the project to be successful, the preservice educators needed to be in communication with the transit agency as well as the newcomer school. Nevertheless, although each group of preservice teachers had a different experience, they all spoke positively about the project and could identify its value in terms of their ability to interact with families in school settings—in spite of linguistic and cultural differences.

Another important aspect related to the project has to do with safety. It is critical for us to ensure the students' safety during the school visit project. To mitigate safety concerns, we incorporated a number of measures. For example, we decided to hold the dinner at a public school next to the apartment complex in order to provide a familiar location for families and students to meet for the first time. In addition, students always worked in pairs. In regard to transportation, the project took advantage of an agreement between the resettlement and the transit agencies, and a transportation agent always accompanied the students and the families to and from the apartment complex. Furthermore, the apartment complex had secured entry. Weekly in-class updates on the project also helped the students anticipate and problem-solve issues as they came up.

In closing, after listening to the students' reflections about the experience, we feel encouraged to continue finding ways of improving our project and expanding opportunities for our students to interact with linguistically and culturally diverse families. In inviting other teacher educators to embrace similar experiences for their students, we close with a remark from one of the students:

> I loved this project. This is my favorite thing I did this year because it was life changing. I feel like it was one of those things that it's not school, if that makes sense .... I felt like it was more of a personal growth than it was taking a class in ESL, and I think that's what learning should be like.

References

Banks, J. A. 2001. *Cultural Diversity and Education*. Boston, MA: Allyn & Bacon.

Erickson, F. 2010. "Culture in Society and in Educational Practices." In *Multicultural Education: Issues and Perspectives*, edited by J. A. Banks and C. A. M. Banks, 7th ed., 33–56. Hoboken, NJ: Wiley.

Freemantle, T. 2012, June 10. "Texas Leads Nation in Refugee Resettlement." *Houston Chronicle*. Accessed January 25, 2013. http://www.chron.com/news/houston-texas/article/Texas-leads-nation-in-refugee-resettlement-3623614.php.

Gahungu, A., O. Gahungu, and F. Luseno. 2011. "Educating Culturally Displaced Students with Truncated Formal Education (CDS-TFE): The Case of Refugee Students and Challenges for Administrators, Teachers, and Counselors." *International Journal of Educational Leadership Preparation* 6 (2): 1–19.

Gay, G. 2010. *Culturally Responsive Teaching: Theory, Research, and Practice*. New York, NY: Teachers College Press.

Gay, G., and K. Kirkland. 2003. "Developing Cultural Critical Consciousness and Self-Reflection in Preservice Teacher Education." *Theory Into Practice* 42 (3): 181–187.

Given, L., ed. 2008. "Narrative Inquiry." In *The Sage Encyclopedia of Qualitative Research Methods*, 541–544. Thousand Oaks, CA: Sage.

Guest, G., K. M. MacQueen, and E. E. Namey. 2011. *Applied Thematic Analysis*. Thousand Oaks, CA: Sage.

Ladson-Billings, G. 1995. "But That's Just Good Teaching! The Case for Culturally Relevant Pedagogy." *Theory Into Practice* 34 (3): 159–165.

Li, G. 2013. "Promoting Teachers of Culturally and Linguistically Diverse (CLD) Students as Change Agents: A Cultural Approach to Professional Learning." *Theory Into Practice* 52 (2): 136–143.

Texas Health and Human Services Commission. (n.d.). *Refugee Resettlement Program*. Accessed January 25, 2013. http://www.hhsc.state.tx.us/programs/refugee/.

FREYCA CALDERON BERUMEN and CECILIA SILVA *are affiliated with Texas Christian University.*

Appendix

List of Internet Resources

- http://www.unhcr.org/cgi-bin/texis/vtx/home
- http://catholiccharitiesfortworth.sitewrench.com/refugeeservices
- http://www.hhsc.state.tx.us/programs/refugee/
- http://www.rescue.org/
- http://www.refugeesinternational.org/
- http://www.migrationinformation.org/usfocus/display.cfm?ID=734
- http://www.refugees.org/our-work/refugee-resettlement/
- http://www.refugees.org/resources/for-refugees--immigrants/cultural-ori entation-resources/
- http://www.acf.hhs.gov/programs/orr
- http://www.acf.hhs.gov/programs/orr/programs/school-impact
- http://www.rcusa.org/index.php?page=history
- http://www.brycs.org/documents/upload/ageandgradeFAQ-3.pdf
- http://www.brycs.org/documents/upload/Collaboration-FAQ-2.pdf
- http://www.brycs.org/documents/upload/ChildWelfare-FAQ.pdf
- http://www.fas.org/sgp/crs/row/R41570.pdf

7

The socially constructed categorization of groups of people has formed perceptions that cause one to believe that being different also means being less than those representing the so-called norm. It is suggested in this chapter that we must broaden our perspectives regarding the differences among us and begin to see each person as an individual with gifts worthy of membership in our society.

Difference Does Not Mean *Less Than*: Our Pathway for Educating an Entire Nation of Learners

Cornell Thomas

We hold these truths to be self-evident, that all men are created equal, that they are endowed by their Creator with certain unalienable Rights that among these are Life, Liberty and the pursuit of Happiness...

> The Declaration of Independence (preamble)

Transgressing Culture Lines (Thomas 2013) is a book that focuses on teaching and learning environments where each student's culture is understood as an individual experience. Nieto (1992) describes culture as:

... the ever changing values, traditions, social and political relationships, and worldview shared by a group of people bound together by a combination of factors that can include a common history, geographic location, language, social class, and/or religion. (306)

Culture is, by this and most definitions today, made up of our background and experiences. While some backgrounds are close to being very similar, our experiences are all different and interpreted in uniquely personal ways. Therefore, it is suggested here that we all have our very own culture, and this culture continues to evolve as we each experience life. Yet

New Directions for Teaching and Learning, no. 140, Winter 2014 © 2014 Wiley Periodicals, Inc.
Published online in Wiley Online Library (wileyonlinelibrary.com) • DOI: 10.1002/tl.20115

the *culture* of our great nation reinforces more of a group identification process full of negative perceptions.

> If we grow up in a culture where we are told that everyone can make it if they try, and yet we can see that many have *not* "made it," and that certain groups are far worse off than others, it becomes almost logical to conclude that there must be something *better* about the groups at the top of the ladder. In other words, the combination of subjective ideology (the myth of meritocracy) and objective inequity (race-based stratification) creates the perfect recipe for the adoption of racist views as well as class bias. That so many of us would fall into that kind of cognitive trap hardly makes us bad people, let alone bigots. (Wise 2012, 69)

So the questions become how do we move away from and remove the cloaking devices protecting and supporting the perpetuation of these kinds of negative and untrue ways of perceiving the world and the people in it?; and what perspectives will move each of us toward positive and more realistic ways of seeing the world and all of the individuals in it? It is suggested here that answers to this second question must guide our work.

> Thomas Jefferson, considered by many scholars in the field to be the father of education in this country, expressed the belief that education would empower individuals to manage their own financial affairs, build morals, realize and act on his/her duties to neighbors and country, and become guardians to their own liberty. W. E. B. Dubois talked about the need for educated African Americans go gain upward mobility in society and as a means of empowerment in the struggle for equality. President Obama believes that it is extremely important to provide the best possible education for every citizen in order for this country to remain a global leader in business, research and the spread of democracy. (Thomas 2013, 90)

With these thoughts in the fore, it seems clear that this work must help us create the kind of pathways that lead to teaching and learning environments where a more educated and thoughtful populace and, therefore, a much stronger nation is the result. Considering this discussion regarding culture, perceptions, and the call for a stronger nation through education, it is suggested here that we travel a different pathway if we truly mean what we say. We must clear away these perceptual barriers as a way to remove the cloaking devices protecting and supporting the perpetuation of these kinds of negative and untrue ways of perceiving the world and the people in it. A way to accomplish this task is to:

• Transgress the markers that frame notions of cultural assimilation.

> Cultural assimilation is the process by which a subaltern group's native language and culture are lost under pressure to assimilate to those of the dominant cultural group. The term is used both to refer to colonized

peoples when dominant colonial states expand into new territories or alternately, when diasporas of immigrants settle into a dominant state society ... Full assimilation occurs when new members of a society become indistinguishable from older members. (en.wikipedia.org/wiki/ Cultural_assimilation)

The socially constructed categorization of groups of people has formed perceptions that cause one to believe that being different also means being less than those representing the so-called *norm*. Traditional values become a way to bring praise to some while subliminally, and outwardly, vilifying the way that others have lived their lives. This way of thinking provides justification for much of the economic, social, and political stratification so prevalent in our country. We must broaden our perspectives regarding the differences among us and stop using these untrue and negative stereotypes to make us feel better about ourselves. It is suggested here that we must move away from attempts to mold others to be *just like us*, to ignore and forget major parts of their identity—their own culture—in order to be included as a full member in our society.

- Transgress the markers that frame notions of cultural tolerance.

Those supporting notions of cultural tolerance point to the need for us to respect our differences. We are called here to respect, accept, and appreciate our different cultural backgrounds. We are called to be proactive in our thoughts and actions when interacting with those who are different. It is said to be an active approach to fight against the many stereotypical beliefs many of us have learned about other groups of people. However, the outcomes of this work seem not to have worked well enough. Interactions are impersonal among those who are different. While we tolerate certain differences among individuals, we do little to embrace *those people* and *their values*. What typically results is often referred to as political correctness. We are polite, courteous, civil, deferential, and sometimes even well mannered—in certain settings. While we are polite, we seldom embrace; we hold otherness at arm's length at best; we keep differences outside of our circle.

- Transgress the markers that frame notions of multiculturalism.

The National Association for Multicultural Education (NAME) provides a detailed definition of multicultural education. In this definition, the Association states:

Multicultural education advocates the belief that students and their life histories and experiences should be placed at the center of the teaching and learning process and that pedagogy should occur in a context that is familiar to students and that addresses multiple ways of thinking ... multicultural education demands a school staff that is culturally competent, and to the greatest extent possible racially, culturally, and linguistically diverse. (NAME Board of Directors 2003)

While I pose no arguments here regarding this description of multi-cultural education, there is great concern for the actions of educators' attempts to embrace this process of teaching and learning. In many school settings, multicultural education has become the practice of acknowledging and respecting the various groups of people in our world. It has resulted in a curriculum that is more student focused, but only in generalized ways. These generalized and often overly very simplified depictions of culture homogenize groups of people and efface individuality and differences that are so important to our identities. The actions that often follow can be seen in school districts across the country; generalizations or best practices to be utilized when working with African American, Hispanic, or other labeled students result in merely surface-level relationships at best. We all understand the value of relationships between students and teachers. It is these relationships that serve as conduits for the connections needed when connecting what students know and the information we want students to learn. One will also note that achievement gaps still persist. The kinds of relationships that develop here between individuals have little chance of developing to their full potential when these generalizations control our thoughts and actions. I often wonder how the relationship I have with my wife would be if I used, for example, the ten best ways to interact with a female. What would be even more problematic would be utilizing the ten best ways to interact with a Black female! This process of teaching and learning is just not enough!

Each generation has made these adjustments and each of us has done the same as new experiences impact our lives. In other words, each person is indeed unique. Each person, to survive, develops their own set of values, beliefs, and ways to navigate the challenges of life. Each person's set of cultural norms evolves as a person lives out his or her life. You see, community is made up of individuals, not groups of people. When we focus on individuals, instead of groups, we are more likely to really get to know someone. We begin to better understand how their gifts can have a positive impact on the community in which we all belong.

Next Step: Connecting

> To transgress culture lines can indeed lead us to positive pathways where high levels of student success are the norm. It can indeed represent a genesis as we create better ways to engage the learner in the teaching and learning process. Our transgressions will empower schools to develop many more thinkers and learners than ever in our history. (Thomas 2013, 102)

Yes, we must transgress the markers that frame notions of assimilation, tolerance, multiculturalism, and any other set of beliefs that create barriers to anything less than the markers that frame the premise of inclusion.

> We are all students. As educators our work calls us to continuously learn how to learn, reflect, discover, grow and share with others. We have dedicated our lives to continuously learn, reflect, grow and improve upon our work. Educators must commit ourselves and take responsibility to clear the pathway of learning and understanding for others as we successfully achieve desired goals. This process of teaching and learning as a practice of freedom encourages us to transgress from where we are perceptually to where we need to go. (Thomas 2013, 4)

The actions taken to embrace the markers that frame inclusion as a way to improve teaching and learning start with an exploration of self by each educator. These actions are counter to most, if not all, approaches to improve teaching and learning in diverse communities of learners. This approach is grounded in the premise that most, if not all, students can learn. Instead of seeing the student from a deficit perspective, the glass (student) half empty, each teacher must unlearn much of what they have been taught and embrace self-exploration as a starting point to improve their craft. This process begins with the premise that the glass (student) is half full and with our assistance will be filled with the kind of knowledge that continues a lifelong journey of exploration and new understandings.

> In many school districts kindergarten students are given a readiness test. This test is basically designed, so they say, to determine the student's readiness to perform the tasks called for by the school's adopted curriculum. How the results are interpreted can often prove to be parts of a strong foundation for connecting what students know to what we want them to learn. On the other hand the interpreted results can prove to be a weak structure upon which instructional designs collapse due to the lack of these much needed connectors. (Thomas 2013, 59)

Is there a pathway or set of beliefs that will lead us away from deficit model teaching? How can we help educators better utilize the knowledge each student brings to the learning environment as a way to foster deeper understanding? What can be done to help teachers internalize the value of connecting the knowledge students possess with the information we want them to learn? What can we provide as a pathway leading to teaching and learning environments that causes each educator to focus on their abilities to connect with all kinds of learners? Is there a set of foundational pillars that we can embrace that will reinforce this work? It is suggested here that we consider Parker Palmer's (2011), in *Healing the Heart of Democracy*, five habits of the heart as the foundational pillars we seek.

> If "We the People" are to hold democracy's tensions in ways that reweave the civic community, we must develop habits that allow our hearts to break open and embrace diversity rather than break down and further divide us. (Palmer 2011, 35)

It is suggested here that these thoughts also inform our teaching and learning communities. Palmer tells us:

- We must understand that we are all in this together (Palmer 2011, 44).

Our weakest area of national defense is quickly becoming an uneducated populace. Therefore, it is in the national interest that we improve what we do in the classroom.

- We must develop an appreciation of the value of "otherness" (Palmer 2011, 44).

We are stronger together than when divided by differences that are seen as *less than*.

- We must cultivate the ability to hold tension in life-giving ways (Palmer 2011, 45).
- We must generate a sense of personal voice and agency (Palmer 2011, 45).

Palmer (2011) tells us, "Democracy gives us the right to disagree and is designed to use the energy of creative conflict to drive social change" (16). This message reinforces the premise that a variety of voices, when included, result in more informed decisions and increases the likelihood of achieving desired outcomes. Teachers must be learners in order to maximize their success with all students. Listen to your students, learn from them. They will show us how to connect with them and what they know.

- We must strengthen our capacity to create community (Palmer 2011, 45).

In this case, I am talking about the school community. A teaching and learning community that believes every person has the ability to learn supports this premise that we are all in this together from a point of strength. In these settings, imagining the possibilities for all learners is the norm. This work supports President Obama's call for every student to graduate from high school prepared for college and/or careers. The focus here is on helping to empower learners to take ownership of every facet of their lives. Teachers focus on the ultimate goal of learners learning how to learn for themselves. What I am referencing here is the ability of each learner to listen intently to knowledge givers. Learners here learn to formulate their own questions as they seek to become more informed citizens. They know how and where to secure information that will increase their bank of knowledge. Learners in teaching and learning environments where stereotypes and preconceived notions of difference are obliterated, transgressing culture lines, create the kinds of environments that result in learners prepared for college, for trade schools, and/or to begin the process of starting their own businesses. These learners are well prepared to imagine their own possibilities and then to turn dreams into reality: A more educated populace, a stronger nation, and a community where every member is included and not thought of as *less than*. "We the People" becomes more of a reality.

References

National Association for Multicultural Education (NAME) Board of Directors. 2003, February. *Definition.* http://www.nameorg.org/resolutions/definition.html.
Nieto, S. 1992. *Affirming Diversity: The Sociopolitical Context of Multicultural Education.* New York, NY: Longman.
Palmer, P. 2011. *Healing the Heart of Democracy: The Courage to Create a Politics Worthy of the Human Spirit.* San Francisco, CA: Jossey-Bass.
Thomas, C. 2013. *Transgressing Culture Lines.* Dubuque, IA: Kendall Hunt.
Wise, T. 2012. *Dear White American.* San Francisco, CA: City Lights Books.

CORNELL THOMAS currently serves as a professor of educational leadership in the College of Education at Texas Christian University.

8

Access to higher education continues to expand in the United States. And, as opportunity has continued to increase, so too has the amount of diversity present throughout higher education. These trends, combined with the fundamental principles connected to the purpose of higher education, work to create culturally relevant and responsive practice. Focused on educational practice designed to meet the needs of a continuously diversifying student population, this chapter examines student programming and curricula as a means to promote student success and learning.

Curriculum Retention and Programming for Inclusive Teaching

Anthony Walker

Introduction

As society continues to become more diverse, the task of educational practitioners to develop learning environments prepared to meet the demands of such a society becomes more daunting (Sen 2005). The task of preparing students to be reflective, reflexive, and responsive leaders is a responsibility of the educational system and practitioners. Ultimately, the establishment of such a culture does not lie in student success on standardized assessments or GPAs but rather, as Carlson (2007) noted, in winning the battle over how people think. Integrating pedagogies of praxis that emphasize teacher empowerment, culturally proficient curricula, and values of inclusiveness creates possibilities to learn by rethinking, reenacting, and ultimately unlearning the many norms that promote inequitable, unjust practice (Carlson 2007). Focused on educational practice that meets the demand and need of students, this chapter examines student programming and curricula as a means to promote student success and learning.

Curricula

Success, in today's state of assessment and accountability, is determined through evaluative measures. According to Neuman (2006), evaluative measures integrate "existing statistics, experimental design, historical

New Directions for Teaching and Learning, no. 140, Winter 2014 © 2014 Wiley Periodicals, Inc.
Published online in Wiley Online Library (wileyonlinelibrary.com) • DOI: 10.1002/tl.20116

documents, or field observations" (543) into data collection processes to assess success. Designed to demonstrate one's accumulation of knowledge, progress, and success, an institution's curriculum is, as Hersh and Merrow (2005) noted, the cornerstone of higher education. As the foundation of practice, curriculum assists in identifying and establishing the values, vision, and goals of an institution, and thus its constituencies. Moreover, through its design and implementation, curriculum provides evidence of an institution's focal points for teaching and learning. Through curricula and teaching, education and its practitioners promote either inequity and marginalization, or inclusiveness and justice (Campbell 2010).

Similar to trends of twenty-first-century society, student bodies throughout higher education continue to diversify. Mission and vision statements, websites, and marketing strategies note institutional values emphasizing practices designed to meet the demands of today's global and interconnected citizenry. However, amid the innumerable publications and postings linking institutional practices with diversity rest curricula that too often continue to reflect philosophical underpinnings manifested in practices that create what Vazquez (1993) alluded to as a propensity for an ideological stasis. Reflective of both tradition and the sustainability of status quos, conventional curricula are often antiquated and unable to engage students in teachings prepared to meet the needs of today's diverse student bodies. Ineffective curricula create a culture of participants by presence only, where, as Harper and Quaye (2009) noted, it is possible to be involved without being engaged.

As the demography of higher education's student body continues to diversify, curriculum reform is necessary. Explaining such need, Gurin et al. (2003) affirmed that without changes to pedagogical practices and theories of thought, education will fail to meet the needs of a citizenry that continues to diversify. Unfortunately, the majority of education holds on to hierarchies of order and practice instead of integrating students' thoughts and perspectives into their practice (Fiore and Rosenquest 2010). Under conventional models, student roles in the design of content, pedagogies, and requirements become passive and disengaged (Fiore and Rosenquest 2010). Aligned more with the system rather than student needs, discourse and dialogue often remain aligned with inadequate, inappropriate pedagogies and practice. In turn, curricula and collegial discourse replace accuracy and evidence with testimonies of ill-advised information that becomes accepted as knowledge (Leonardo 2004). Further, when fixed in ideals and standards of accountability, empowerment and critical thinking become upstaged by a focus on controlling the mind by governing what is taught and learned (Pinar 2012).

Although traditional forms of education often fail to integrate culturally proficient, responsive pedagogies into practice, evidence of progress and opportunity does exist. Such change begins with the establishment of curricula that embrace the student body served by the institution (Fiore and

Rosenquest 2010). With curricula being a complicated dialogue between students and teachers (Pinar 2012), hierarchies of educational practice that place students as secondary participants inhibit both teaching and learning. However, when a curriculum endorses student engagement and needs, practice reflects a constant ebb and flow of thoughts established by experiences of past, meanings of the present, and visions for the future (Pinar 2012).

A curriculum built for the integration of students' thoughts and experiences has the ability to create a learning environment in which students are connected and engaged (Nieto 2004). Involved in determining the content of their schooling, conversations can be framed around deconstructing the who, what, when, where, why, and how of students' learning and growth (Fiore and Rosenquest 2010). It is through such practice that education, being responsible for student learning (Campbell 2010) and service for the public good (Kezar 2005), is able to apply just, equitable pedagogies to promote student-focused, learning-centered curricula and programming.

Programming

Instead of addressing potential causes for pitfalls in student performances, discussions about success in higher education have traditionally placed accountability on students. However, as campuses continue to change, conversations about accountability and responsibility do as well. With increases in assessment and tracking, research now emphasizes the role that educational experiences and teachings play in student success in higher education. Discussing issues related to difficulties in the high school to college transition, Zamani (2000) pointed to relationships between inadequate experiences and learning prior to their collegiate endeavors. According to her, examinations into the backgrounds of many students enrolled in institutions of higher education demonstrate that disconnects between students and institutions are often present before a student arrives on campus (Zamani 2000).

Perspectives and arguments such as Zamani's, which place weight on the ineffectiveness of the education system, counter historical trends and data sets arguing that low retention rates are often the result of inadequate intellectual abilities set to reinforce traditional research. However, as Cabrera et al. (1999) noted, socially constructed norms leading to negative perceptions, low expectations, and discrimination have negative impacts on student experiences and success. Further, as noted by Jones (2001), research demonstrates links between student success and institutional factors such as campus climate, curricula, and programming. Supported by research such as Cabrera et al.'s (1999) and Jones's (2001), changes in perspective, perception, and debate allow for modifications in discussions tending to the topics of student persistence, achievement gaps, and the overall effectiveness within higher education in the United States.

Students are, without a doubt, the most important stakeholders for institutions of higher education (Dhanuja 2012). However, equipped with life's baggage, students bring a personalized history of culture, experiences, teachings, and learning with them to college. Accompanied with baggage of life lessons, many students experience feelings of bewilderment, cultural disconnectedness, and trepidation on college campuses (Jehangir 2009). In turn, detachments between individual and institutional backgrounds often create cultures that fail to establish learning environments conducive to meeting the needs of an institution's most important stakeholders: the students. Void of student input and perspectives, such practice creates a culture of disengagement and disinterest. And, as Pinar (2012) highlighted, disconnects between students and curricula ensure a "failure to learn" (Chapter 1, paragraph 9). It is for these reasons and more that, as Buultjens and Robinson (2011) highlighted, how institutions provide student services and programs is crucial.

Although effective learning and teaching are the result of a quality curriculum (Surapur 2013), traditional practice and programming tend to create what Brown and Ratcliff (1998) noted as "fragmented curricular and campus programming" (18). Disjointed and inequitable, programming too often relegates learning to cultures and learning styles conducive to prevailing norms and practices. However, even amid customs of ineffective, marginalizing practice, solutions for progressive, equitable programming lie in higher education's core responsibility of serving students for the betterment of the public good. Premised in service to its constituencies, curricula that are inclusive and diverse increase the effectiveness of an institution's teaching, learning, and practice (Kumashiro 2003). It is through an investment in values of equity and inclusiveness that programs become more than the passing of information from practitioner to student. Instead, programming becomes a comprehensive cycle of design, implementation, and assessment. Based on principles of learning and meeting student needs, programs and curricula are constantly morphing, changing with student and institutional needs.

Example of Practice

Throughout my career in academia, I have had the fortune to serve many students from many different backgrounds and cultures. For example, I have worked at public and private; two-year and four-year; predominantly White and minority serving institutions; land grant, liberal arts, and research universities; as well as institutions of higher education with enrollments ranging from 600 to more than 24,000 students. Included in these experiences is a focus on working with students to both influence and impact learning and success through effective, effectual programming. Regardless of my position or responsibility, one constant has remained in my practice:

students. Student needs, learning, and success have been, are, and will remain the driving forces behind my practice.

In my experiences, systematic processes of data collection (Gay, Mills, and Airasian 2009) often correlate to tellers of success, for both students and institutions. With grade point averages, persistence, and graduation rates representing aspects of success, quantitative data often become the communicator of results linked to programs and services. However, such measures do not guarantee an insight into the processes involved in the achievement of results. Gauging the success of programs and program curricula requires more than a series of results-oriented, quantitative data. Instead, effective, holistic evaluations of student success include, as Stake (2004) illustrated, connections with both qualitative and quantitative data that include both critical, objective measurements and subjective perceptions. Further, the very nature of curricula, being a complicated dialogue between students and teachers (Pinar 2012), highlights deficiencies in student success measures that are void of qualitative data.

My career in academia includes a tenure working at a large, public institution located in the Midwest Region of the United States. Both a land grant and research university, Midwest University (MU) was also historically and predominantly White. Serving the institution, I worked within MU's Office of Diversity and Inclusion (ODI) where my primary responsibilities focused on implementing the First Year Success (FYS) Program, an initiative designed to increase retention rates of first-year students from diverse backgrounds. It was during the initial phase of my work at MU that I became introduced to two topics that would both guide and transform my philosophy and practice. Those topics were privilege and critical theory. As I became more knowledgeable of each, my practice evolved and my approaches to the design of student services fused values of criticality with curricula to establish what Surapur (2013) defined as an effective curriculum that was engaged with student needs (Pinar 2012).

Equipped with a budding knowledge base and heightened sense of awareness, I introduced principles of criticality into the design of FYS and set out to develop a curriculum that was student-centered, inclusive, and prepared to meet the diverse needs of the students I served. Being new to campus, becoming familiar with the various cultures within MU was imperative to my practice. Therefore, initial planning dealt with establishing the purpose, objectives, and assessment measures for FYS. Meetings with multiple stakeholders representing numerous constituencies across campus became routine throughout the summer months preceding my first academic semester. Building networks and developing relationships across campus, my knowledge and awareness of MU grew, as did ideas and possibilities for how to implement FYS. Therefore, using the institutional vision and mission, along with the knowledge gained from meetings and discussions with MU personnel, I established a framework for the implementation of FYS.

New Directions for Teaching and Learning • DOI: 10.1002/tl

Although I was becoming acquainted with MU's culture, and I designed a general context for FYS, my knowledge primarily reflected the perspectives of MU's faculty and staff. In turn, my efforts were limited as FYS's content and context lacked input from what Dhanuja (2012) identified as an institution's most important stakeholders: the students. My planning failed to integrate thoughts, perspectives, and experiences of students, thus not ensuring a connectedness and engagement with students (Nieto 2004). Acknowledging the need to integrate students into the planning, implementation, and assessment of FYS, I then focused on creating a balance between theory and practice as I moved forward with my work.

Equipped with a personalized understanding of MU's culture and vision, at the start of the academic year, I met with students. With an outline of FYS prepared, the meeting focused on collecting feedback from students and discussing ways to incorporate a program that met the needs of both the students and FYS. Engaged in conversations focused on how, what, when, and where FYS would be implemented, the development of FYS's curriculum was exactly as Pinar (2012) described, a complicated conversation with students.

Connected to both theory and experience, FYS quickly transitioned from a curriculum on paper to a program in action. Critical in theory, practical in design, FYS quickly proved a success. Led by a focus on integrating students' perspective into the design and implementation, FYS grew in participation and engagement. And, recognizing that student needs change as he or she adapts to life as a college student, a dialogue focused on ways to improve the program remained a constant. Whether the need for change came mid-semester or mid-year, being engaged and in tune with the students, I was able to adjust FYS's curriculum, design, and implementation without sacrificing the program philosophy, purpose, or objectives. What culminated was a program that became known among faculty, staff, and students as a program that integrated a comprehensive approach to student success. What resulted was a program and curriculum that remained engaged, up to date with trends, and prepared to meet student needs. Engaged, relevant, and focused on students, the success of FYS was evident throughout campus. Each semester, data demonstrated increases in success based on retention, GPAs, and campus engagement with program GPAs and retention data highlighting success rates higher than their peers not involved in FYS.

Conclusion

Institutions of higher education continue to change and become more diverse (Elam and Brown 2005). However, the fundamental task of higher education to serve the public (Kezar 2005) remains. The Kellogg Commission (2000) acknowledged similar testaments in its reporting that higher education is responsible for the advancement and progress of society. Believing that few would argue the purpose or responsibility higher education has to both students and greater society, for me, the debate then becomes what does such service look like and how do institutions of higher education go about the task of performing such responsibilities.

As colleges and universities continue to invest resources into efforts to enhance support services, the attention to student success is evident. The task then, as Sen (2005) discussed, is to develop learning environments that are prepared to meet the demands of a diverse, interconnected society (122). An investment in fulfilling the responsibility to serve and propel the citizenry forward (The Kellogg Commission 2000; Kezar 2005) is imperative to the success of both higher education and society. For, as Morey (2000) explained, a failure to integrate culturally proficient pedagogies into curriculum and programming will limit higher education's ability to meet the needs of both students and society. Equipped with the knowledge and resources, higher education has the tools required to integrate pedagogies of praxis that are equitable, inclusive, and prepared to serve for betterment of the public good.

References

Brown, M. C., and J. L. Ratcliff. 1998. "Multiculturalism and Multicultural Curricula in the United States." *Higher Education in Europe* 23 (1): 11–21.

Buultjens, M., and P. Robinson. 2011. "Enhancing Aspects of the Higher Education Student Experience." *Journal of Higher Education Policy and Management* 33 (4): 337–346.

Cabrera, A. F., A. Nora, P. T. Terenzini, E. Pascarella, and L. S. Hagedorn. 1999. "Campus Racial Climate and the Adjustment of Students of College." *The Journal of Higher Education* 79 (2): 134–160.

Campbell, D. E. 2010. *Choosing Democracy: A Practical Guide to Multicultural Education*, 4th ed. Boston, MA: Pearson Education.

Carlson, D. 2007. "Are We Making Progress: The Discursive Construction of Progress in the Age of No Child Left Behind." In *Keeping the Promise: Essays on Leadership, Democracy, and Education*, edited by D. Carlson and P. Gause, 3–26. New York, NY: Peter Lang Publishing.

Dhanuja, R. 2012. "Contribution of Students Towards Enhancing Quality in Higher Education Institutions." *Indian Streams Research Journal* 2 (11): 1–6.

Elam, C., and G. Brown. 2005. "The Inclusive University: Helping Students Choose a College and Identify Institutions that Value Diversity." *Journal of College Admission* 187: 14–17.

Fiore, L., and B. Rosenquest. 2010. "Shifting the Culture of Higher Education: Influences of Students, Teachers, and Pedagogy." *Theory into Practice* 49 (1): 14–20.

Gay, L. R., G. E. Mills, and P. W. Airasian. 2009. *Educational Research: Competencies for Analysis and Applications*, 9th ed. Columbus, OH: Prentice-Hall.

Gurin, P., E. L. Dey, S. Hurtado, and G. Gurin. 2003. "Diversity and Higher Education: Theory and Impact on Educational Outcomes." In *Race and Higher Education: Rethinking Pedagogy in Diverse College Classrooms*, edited by A. Howell and F. Tuitt, 9–42. Cambridge, MA: Harvard Education Publishing Group.

Harper, S. R., and S. J. Quaye. 2009. "Beyond Sameness with Engagement and Outcomes for All: An Introduction." In *Student Engagement in Higher Education: Theoretical Perspectives and Practical Approaches for Diverse Populations* [Kindle iPad version], edited by S. R. Harper and S. J. Quaye, 1–16. New York, NY: Routledge.

Hersh, R. H., and J. Merrow. 2005. *Declining by Degrees: Higher Education at Risk.* New York, NY: Palgrave MacMillan.

Jehangir, R. R. 2009. "Cultivating Voice: First Generation Students Seek Full Academic Citizenship in Multicultural Learning Communities." *Innovative Higher Education* 34: 33–49.

Jones, L. 2001. "Creating an Affirming Culture to Retain African American Students During the Postaffirmative Action Era in Higher Education." In *Retaining African Americans in Higher Education: Challenging Paradigms for Retaining Students, Faculty, and Administrators,* edited by L. Jones, 3–20. Sterling, VA: Stylus.

The Kellogg Commission. 2000. *Returning to Our Roots: The Engaged Institution (3rd report). Kellogg Commission on the Future of State and Land-Grant Institutions.* New York, NY: National Association of State Universities and Land-Grant Colleges.

Kezar, A. J. 2005. "Challenges for Higher Education in Serving the Public Good." In *Higher Education for the Public Good: Emerging Voices from a National Movement,* edited by A. J. Kezar, T. C. Chambers, J. C. Burkhardt, and Associates, 23–42. San Francisco, CA: Jossey-Bass.

Kumashiro, K. K. 2003. "Against Repetition: Addressing Resistance to Anti-oppressive Change in the Practices of Learning, Teaching, Supervising, and Researching." In *Race and Higher Education: Rethinking Pedagogy in Diverse College Classrooms,* edited by A. Howell and F. Tuitt, 45–67. Cambridge, MA: Harvard Education Publishing Group.

Leonardo, Z. 2004. "The Color of Supremacy: Beyond the Discourse of 'White Privilege.'" *Educational Philosophy and Theory* 36 (2): 137–152.

Morey, A. I. 2000. "Changing Higher Education Curricula for a Global and Multicultural World." *Higher Education in Europe* 25 (1): 25–39.

Neuman, W. L. 2006. *Social Research Methods: Qualitative and Quantitative Approaches,* 6th ed. Boston, MA: Pearson Education.

Nieto, S. 2004. *Affirming Diversity: The Sociopolitical Context of Multicultural Education,* 4th ed. Boston, MA: Pearson Education.

Pinar, W. F. 2012. *What Is Curriculum Theory,* 2nd ed. New York, NY: Routledge.

Sen, S. 2005. "Diversity and North American Planning Curricula: The Need for Reform." *Canadian Journal of Urban Research* 14 (1): 121–144.

Stake, R. E. 2004. *Standards Based and Responsive Evaluation.* Thousands Oak, CA: Sage.

Surapur, A. B. 2013. "The Learning Community and Teaching Strategies." *Indian Streams Research Journal* 3 (3): 1–6.

Vazquez, J. M. 1993. "Multiculturalism in the University: Consultation, Advocacy, and the Politics of Culture." *Journal of Educational and Psychological Consultation* 4 (3): 215–235.

Zamani, E. M. 2000. "Sources and Information Regarding Effective Retention Strategies for Students of Color." In *Beyond Access: Methods and Models for Increasing Retention and Learning among Minority Students,* New Directions for Community Colleges, no. 112, edited by S. R. Aragon, 95–104. San Francisco, CA: Jossey-Bass.

ANTHONY WALKER *is the director of Student Success and Completion at Tarrant County College and an adjunct professor at Texas Christian University.*

Index

NEW DIRECTIONS FOR TEACHING AND LEARNING
ORDER FORM SUBSCRIPTION AND SINGLE ISSUES

DISCOUNTED BACK ISSUES:

Use this form to receive 20% off all back issues of *New Directions for Teaching and Learning*.
All single issues priced at **$23.20** (normally $29.00)

TITLE	ISSUE NO.	ISBN

Call 1-800-835-6770 or see mailing instructions below. When calling, mention the promotional code JBNND to receive your discount. For a complete list of issues, please visit www.josseybass.com/go/ndtl

SUBSCRIPTIONS: (1 YEAR, 4 ISSUES)

☐ New Order   ☐ Renewal

U.S.	☐ Individual: $89	☐ Institutional: $335
Canada/Mexico	☐ Individual: $89	☐ Institutional: $375
All Others	☐ Individual: $113	☐ Institutional: $409

Call 1-800-835-6770 or see mailing and pricing instructions below.
Online subscriptions are available at www.onlinelibrary.wiley.com

ORDER TOTALS:

Issue / Subscription Amount: $ _____

Shipping Amount: $ _____
(for single issues only – subscription prices include shipping)

Total Amount: $ _____

SHIPPING CHARGES:

First Item	$6.00
Each Add'l Item	$2.00

(No sales tax for U.S. subscriptions. Canadian residents, add GST for subscription orders. Individual rate subscriptions must be paid by personal check or credit card. Individual rate subscriptions may not be resold as library copies.)

BILLING & SHIPPING INFORMATION:

☐ **PAYMENT ENCLOSED:** *(U.S. check or money order only. All payments must be in U.S. dollars.)*

☐ **CREDIT CARD:** ☐ VISA ☐ MC ☐ AMEX

Card number _____ Exp. Date _____

Card Holder Name _____ Card Issue # _____

Signature _____ Day Phone _____

☐ **BILL ME:** *(U.S. institutional orders only. Purchase order required.)*

Purchase order # _____
Federal Tax ID 13559302 • GST 89102-8052

Name _____

Address _____

Phone _____ E-mail _____

Copy or detach page and send to: **John Wiley & Sons, One Montgomery Street, Suite 1000, San Francisco, CA 94104-4594**

Order Form can also be faxed to: **888-481-2665**

PROMO JBNND